Winning Grants

Step by Step

Winning Grants

Step by Step

THIRD EDITION

Mim Carlson, Tori O'Neal-McElrath,
and the Alliance for Nonprofit Management

JOSSEY-BASS
A Wiley Imprint
www.josseybass.com

Published by Jossey-Bass
A Wiley Imprint
989 Market Street, San Francisco, CA 94103-1741—www.josseybass.com

Jossey-Bass books and products are available through most bookstores. To contact Jossey-Bass directly call our Customer Care Department within the U.S. at 800-956-7739, outside the U.S. at 317-572-3986, or fax 317-572-4002.

Jossey-Bass also publishes its books in a variety of electronic formats. Some content that appears in print may not be available in electronic books.

Library of Congress Cataloging-in-Publication Data
Carlson, Mim.
  Winning grants step by step / Mim Carlson and Tori O'Neal-McElrath. — 3rd ed.
     p. cm. — (The Jossey-Bass nonprofit guidebook series)
  Includes bibliographical references and index.
  ISBN 978-0-470-28637-1 (pbk.)
  1. Proposal writing for grants. 2. Nonprofit organizations—Finance. I. O'Neal-McElrath, Tori. II. Title.
  HG177.C374 2008
  658.15'224—dc22

                                                                                        2008022741

Printed in the United States of America
THIRD EDITION
PB Printing   10 9 8 7 6 5 4 3 2 1

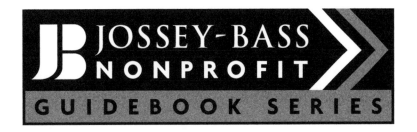

The Jossey-Bass Nonprofit Guidebook Series

The Jossey-Bass Nonprofit Guidebook Series provides new to experienced nonprofit professionals and volunteers with the essential tools and practical knowledge they need to make a difference in the world. From hands-on workbooks to step-by-step guides on developing a critical skill or learning how to perform an important task or process, our accomplished expert authors provide readers with the information required to be effective in achieving goals, mission, and impact.

Other Titles in The Jossey-Bass Nonprofit Guidebook Series

Contents

List of Samples, Worksheets, and Figures

CD Contents

Acknowledgments

THIS WORKBOOK IS a coming together of all aspects of the nonprofit sector involved in grantseeking and grantmaking. Nonprofit staff and volunteers, intermediary organizations like the Alliance serving nonprofits, consultants both seasoned and new, and representatives of grantmaking institutions all had a hand in this workbook. It represents collaboration at its best. In this third edition, *Winning Grants Step by Step* will continue to augment the many workshops and clinics and the various forms of consultation available on proposal writing. Thanks are due to the many people who contributed directly and indirectly to this edition, both those involved primarily with grantseeking and those who are grantmakers.

Several individuals deserve special mention. The primary author of the first and second editions of this book, Mim Carlson, is the executive director of the Berkeley–East Bay Humane Society. In her prior work as a nonprofit management consultant and manager, she reviewed hundreds of proposals in her thirty-plus years of working in the sector. She has also taught proposal writing in nonprofit certificate courses at universities throughout the San Francisco Bay Area. The Alliance for Nonprofit Management is indebted to Mim for authoring two stellar editions of this workbook.

For this third edition of *Winning Grants Step by Step*, the Alliance decided to bring in an additional voice, that of Tori O'Neal-McElrath, to both amplify Mim's tried-and-true advice and offer new information based on changes in the grantsmanship field. Tori is an organizational development consultant with over nineteen years of combined experience on both sides of the philanthropic coin; she has worked with and for both grantseeking and grantmaking organizations. She has also taught fundraising courses in nonprofit certificate courses in Southern California, as well as numerous workshops, seminars, and conferences nationwide. Tori graciously agreed to step up and take the lead on this latest revision, given Mim's shift to focus on her work as an executive director as well as her writing of the second edition of *The Executive Director's Survival Guide.* The resulting combination of voices has undoubtedly increased this workbook's usefulness. The Alliance appreciates Tori's work and leadership on this new edition.

Several individuals made significant contributions to the first edition that have been carried through in the second and now the third editions of this workbook. Jan Masaoka, former executive director of CompassPoint Nonprofit Services; Jane Arsenault, former executive director of the Support Center of Rhode Island; and Rick Smith, formerly the national executive director of the Support Centers of America, deserve continued acknowledgment for their time and energy. Much of what they contributed to the first edition appears—in whole or in part—in sections of this workbook, proof that good work does live on.

Special acknowledgments specific to this third edition go to a few extraordinary individuals, who were also strong devotees of the first and second editions of this workbook. Sheryl Kaplan, a fifteen-year veteran as a grantwriting consultant, provided invaluable feedback throughout the writing of this workbook. She also contributed several sample proposals for successfully funded grants, which can be found on the CD. Deanna Campbell is a relatively new grantwriter who contributed greatly to this edition by asking just the right clarifying questions. Olga Castenada also contributed guidance in the refinement of the sample project used throughout the workbook, as well as contributed a sample capacity-building grant proposal.

Phyllis Caldwell, Julie Farkas, Desiree Flores, Valerie Jacobs, Sandi Jibrell, Edward Kacic, Gwen Walden, and Susan Zepeda all provided keen insights into the grantmaking process, based on their years of experience; many of these wonderful insights have been quoted to expand and enhance many of the major points made about the steps described in this workbook. Through meetings, e-mail exchanges, and phone calls, they were both generous and thought provoking in turn about what they hoped would be conveyed in this edition of the workbook, which was more context for the grantmaking process itself—in addition to the nuts-and-bolts information on proposal development—so that grantseekers could gain an even greater understanding of all the activities involved. They also gave of their time— a precious commodity in the grantmaking arena. Please pay particular attention to what they have shared in their own words, and use their words of experience to inform your own grantseeking efforts.

The Authors

MIM CARLSON has served as executive director of the Berkeley–East Bay Humane Society for the past four years. She has worked in the nonprofit sector for over twenty-five years as an executive director, interim director, and consultant for several animal welfare groups and social services organizations. She is a member of the executive committee of her county's advisory council on aging and has served on numerous nonprofit boards of directors. She is also the coauthor of *The Executive Director's Survival Guide* and the author of two books, *Winning Grants Step by Step* (first and second editions) and *Team-Based Fundraising Step by Step*, all published by Jossey-Bass.

TORI O'NEAL-McELRATH has more than nineteen years' experience in the areas of fundraising, program design and implementation, and organizational development capacity building with a broad range of foundations and community-based agencies. As the principal of O'Neal Consulting Services since 2000, Tori specializes in multifunder collaborations, board development, and capacity building in all areas of fundraising, strategic planning, and direct technical assistance. Her clients have included The Partnership for Prince George's County (Maryland), Health Funders Partnership of Orange County (California), Women & Philanthropy (Washington, D.C.), Washington Area Women's Foundation (Washington, D.C.), and Planned Parenthood of Orange & San Bernardino Counties (California), to name a few. She has successfully raised millions of dollars from foundations, corporations, and individuals throughout her years as a consultant, staff person, board member, and volunteer. Tori taught major gifts fundraising while on the faculty of UCLA Extension in 1996 and is in frequent demand as a speaker at conferences and workshops.

About the Alliance for Nonprofit Management

The Alliance for Nonprofit Management is the professional association of individuals and organizations devoted to improving the management and governance capacity of nonprofits to assist nonprofits in fulfilling their mission. The Alliance is a learning community that promotes quality in nonprofit capacity building. The Alliance convenes a major annual conference, networks colleagues year-round online, and provides member discounts on books and other publications. Visit us online at www.allianceonline.org.

How to Use This Workbook: Making the "Magic" Happen

WINNING GRANTS Step by Step will walk you through, step by step as the title implies, the basic grantwriting process and will clearly illustrate that doing your research up front, following directions, building relationships, and implementing sound program planning is what actually makes the magic happen. By employing the strategies as outlined, you will significantly increase your ability to turn organizational programs, projects, and even general operating needs into proposals worthy of the full consideration of funders.

This is a hands-on, user-friendly workbook that guides you through the various stages of development that will enable you to take an idea or concept and make it come to life on paper. Real-life examples, samples of materials, worksheets to support you as you create your own materials, and helpful tips can be found throughout the workbook, and are tailored specifically step by step. Guidelines, suggestions, and exercises will prepare you to tackle proposal development for various organizations in the nonprofit arena—community-based agencies, educational institutions, hospitals and clinics, and research organizations. "Reality Checks" and "Helpful Hints" offer brief focused guidance. "Definitions," unless otherwise stated, are provided by the Nonprofit Good Practice Guide (www.npgoodpractice.org/Glossary), a project of the Johnson Center at Grand Valley State University.

Ultimately, the worksheets and other activities in this workbook are crafted to assist you in developing your proposals and letters of inquiry to meet the requirements of funding institutions of various types—corporate, private, operating, family, and community. (See Resource A at the end of the workbook for definitions of each type of foundation.)

Winning Grants Step by Step has been crafted with three kinds of individuals in mind: (1) entry-level grantwriters, (2) other organizational staff and volunteers with limited knowledge or experience of grantwriting, and (3) people with some experience who are seeking a refresher in "Grantwriting 101." Though grantwriting basics can be generally applied to all types of grant processes, this workbook focuses primarily on foundation and corporate grants, although there are several government funding resources provided in the Special Resources Section. If you are seeking more guidance on government grants (also referred to as public funding), you might want to check out *Grant Writing for Dummies,* by Bev Browning, which offers chapters specifically dedicated to government funding. Additionally, those of you working in the area of achieving social justice through grassroots organizations face unique challenges specific to your work. You will certainly find parts of *Winning Grants Step by Step* useful, but you might also want to check out *Grassroots Grants: An Activist's Guide to Grantseeking,* by Andy Robinson. It does a highly effective job of tailoring the grantseeking process to meet the needs of grassroots organizations working for social justice.

This workbook is modeled on creating proposals for program funding, and you can easily adapt it to seek general support and other types of funding as well. *Winning Grants Step by Step* targets this basic truth: your proposal must clearly articulate a well thought out, well-crafted program that both inspires confidence in your nonprofit's ability to successfully implement it and fits within the interests of the funders who will receive it. Funders are looking to make strategic investments with their limited grant resources, and they need to see a direct connection between your program and community need(s) being met—and they need to see how you will track and measure your success.

Almost every organization out there addressing community needs has good ideas. The key to winning grants is to match those good ideas with funders who are interested in the same actions and outcomes.

Step One of this workbook walks you through the process of developing a proposal idea.

Step Two provides guidance on introducing your project to possible funders, as well as some helpful ideas about ways to develop relationships with funders, which is a critical component in winning grants.

Steps Three through Ten focus on the specific process components that will take your idea from a concept to an effective proposal.

Then Step Eleven walks you through the final step in the process, submitting your proposal.

Step Twelve focuses on how to sustain relationships with funders after the grantmaking process has concluded—whether your program was funded or not.

Reality Check

In the spirit of David Letterman's nightly "Top Ten," here are arguably the "Top Five" flaws found in grantseekers' proposals:

No. 5.   Failing to work out an appropriate budget for the proposed program. You can hit a home run with your proposal only to have it fall to the ground when it becomes clear that you did not spend enough time and thought on the corresponding program budget.

No. 4.   Underestimating the importance of addressing sustainability. Funders want to make investments, and most would like to think that their investments will have a payoff that extends beyond the life of their grants.

No. 3.   Underplaying the importance—and the significance—of evaluation. Funders want to see that you began with the end in mind; your organization first understood the need, then created a program or project to address that need.

No. 2.   Not being clear enough about what they are trying to achieve through their proposed program or project. Why is your program important for your community or target audience? What—or who—will be different as a result of your program, and how?

No. 1.   The number one flaw grantseekers make is a simple one: not following the funder's grant guidelines. This is an important point that will be emphasized throughout the workbook.

Finally, the Special Resource Section at the end of the workbook addresses key components of the grantseeking process, such as prospect research, and offers a bibliography of directories and guides to advanced proposal development and a list of helpful websites.

Incorporated throughout *Winning Grants Step by Step* are samples that highlight what a particular step is addressing. These samples focus on the work of the Some City Senior Center organization, which provides health and social services to seniors. Some City Senior Center is similar to a real-life organization, and its Senior Latino Community Outreach Pilot Project is also representative of the real organization.

Additional sample proposals are included on the CD-ROM that accompanies this book. You will find examples of capacity building, program, and technology equipment proposals. All these proposals were funded. Each proposal is unique to the organization for which it was written, and is meant to be used only as a demonstration of how the different components can be crafted. The CD-ROM also contains the worksheets from the book that display the CD-ROM icon. (These worksheet files may be filled out electronically or used as templates, to be customized as needed.) Further information on how to run the CD-ROM is located at the end of this book.

The best way to use *Winning Grants Step by Step* is to actually go through it step by step, in the order suggested, crafting your own grant proposal along the way. This workbook is unique because it is structured to follow the process normally used when preparing a proposal; you can develop a proposal of your own as you read the book and complete the exercises.

Remember, there is no magic to navigating the grantseeking process or to preparing successful proposals. These activities simply take good planning, good writing, good research, and an approach that is geared to a prospective funder with whom you have developed a good relationship.

Winning Grants

Step by Step

Introduction

An Overview of the Grantseeking Process

THERE'S NO DENYING IT: grants are an excellent source of support for both emerging and established nonprofit organizations. They are relatively inexpensive compared to other fundraising efforts, though grantseeking often requires a significant amount of dedicated staff time and attention to detail if it is to be done well. A strong proposal—that is, a well-written, well-organized, and concise proposal—can bring in substantial income for your program.

However, before you start on the path of seeking grant funding, you need to ask, *Is my organization ready for grant funding?* Briefly answer these four sets of questions:

1. Are my organization's mission, purpose, and goals already well established and articulated? Do we have a strategic plan or operational plan in place?

2. Does my organization have financial procedures in place? Do we have the ability to effectively track and monitor how we spend grant funds?

3. Do we have the needed staff in place to ensure that we can do what we promise? After all, a grant proposal is a contract. If not, do we have the ability to get the right staff in place quickly and effectively if we are awarded a grant?

4. Are we prepared to do what it takes to meet the requirements that come with receiving grant funding? These requirements might include some or all of the following: producing quarterly, semiannual, or annual progress reports (including financial updates relative to the grant); conducting ongoing program evaluation; participating in special training; and attending conferences and meetings (particularly if the funding relates to a special initiative of a foundation). Meeting

grant expectations might also require us to expand our services, increase our office space, and support staff expansion (with human resources efforts, information technology, and training).

If you answered yes to these four groups of questions, your organization is most likely ready to begin the grantseeking process.

In many instances a well-prepared and clearly articulated proposal can build your organization's credibility with grantmakers, whether you are initially successful in securing a grant or not. Nonprofits that have the respect of grantmakers are often proactively sought after to work on issues of particular concern to both themselves and the funders. Often this funder solicitation comes in the form of a targeted funder initiative. This provides both the grantmaker and the nonprofit with a unique opportunity to collaborate on a larger scale than they would under an individual grant.

Grantwriting is, naturally, a popular way for nonprofits to secure funding for programs; however, it is but one of several ways your organization can raise funds. There are many different fund development campaigns that might increase revenues—and visibility—for your organization, including (but not limited to) direct-mail and e-mail efforts, membership drives, special events, donor giving clubs, online giving drives, "thons" (as in walk-a-thons, dance-a-thons, and jump-a-thons), and more. These should all be kept in mind in addition to grantseeking as a part of a well-rounded fundraising plan. Not only is a well-rounded fundraising plan something grantmakers like to see, but it is vital to a nonprofit's ongoing work, as gaining support is important to build shared ownership in the nonprofit by constituents and other supporters, so it remains well grounded. Also, grantseeking is a process that takes time. Some grant cycles take as much as six months from the time you submit a proposal to the time you learn whether it has been funded. Then, if your organization is awarded a grant, it might take up to another three months before you actually get the check. If your organization is in need of immediate funds, writing a proposal is typically not the most effective way to raise the money.

Nonprofit organizations have seen some fairly significant shifts in the funding climate over the last few years, but one thing remains the same: the vast majority of the funds raised in the private sector come from *individuals*, not foundations. The chart in Figure I.1 illustrates this point.

Government funding, delivered through grants from federal, state, and local agencies, adds billions of public dollars that are not factored into the chart in Figure I.1. That said, government funds are typically offered for projects aimed at very narrow target audiences and qualifications, so make sure you read the fine print before you spend the time—and it will take some time—completing government agencies' grant applications.

Figure I.1

2006 Charitable Giving: Total = $295.02 Billion

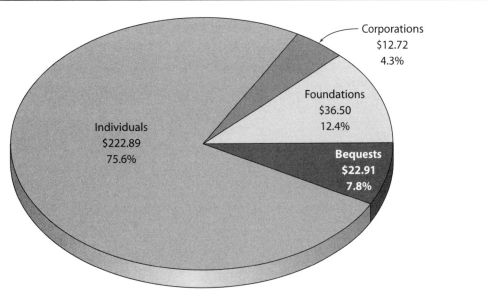

Corporations
$12.72
4.3%

Foundations
$36.50
12.4%

Individuals
$222.89
75.6%

Bequests
$22.91
7.8%

Source: Giving USA Foundation, *Giving USA 2007: The Annual Report on Philanthropy for the Year 2006.* Glenview, Ill.: Giving USA Foundation, 2007.

Reality Check

Some foundations are directing a growing percentage of their grants to larger organizations (national nonprofits, those with affiliates, universities, hospitals, museums, and the like). This makes the competition particularly stiff if your organization is relatively small (under $1 million). This is all the more reason to state your organization's case clearly throughout your proposal.

Categories of Support

Organizations are dynamic and have varied financial needs, which typically fall into one of the following categories:

- *Operating* (general support or unrestricted income). This is the funding your nonprofit needs to pay rent, utilities, and the other everyday costs associated with running the organization—the basics that allow it to fulfill its mission. Typically, the sources of general operating funds are individuals (through annual fund campaigns, direct-mail campaigns, and special events), earned income, and grants.

- *Program* (temporarily restricted income). Program or special project funding is of primary interest to most grantmakers, be they foundations, corporations, or even government agencies. It is funding that your organization receives to start a new program, run or expand an existing program, or launch a time-limited project.

- *Capacity building.* This special project funding is used for a targeted effort to increase your organization's capacity to better support its mission and fulfill its particular administrative or fundraising goals. Over the last few years, foundations in particular have become much more willing—in fact some are even eager—to invest in capacity-building grants to organizations doing great work.

- *Capital or equipment.* Funds for capital support are often raised through a targeted fundraising drive known as a capital campaign or through seeking special equipment grants. These intensive efforts—designed to generate a specified amount of funds within a specified time period for construction, remodeling and renovation, building expansion, or the purchase of land or equipment—typically involve large-scale individual major gift solicitations, followed by substantial support from foundations and corporations. Some government agencies also provide funds for capital projects.

- *Endowments.* Funds for endowments are often generated through bequests and planned gifts, that is, through giving by an individual to an organization under the terms of a will or trust. Endowment funds may also be received as part of a capital or endowment campaign, using the methods for raising capital or equipment funds. In some cases a longtime funder dedicated to your cause may be willing to make an endowment grant, which may be a way to solidify their support of your nonprofit, or may be a part of an exit strategy on the part of the grantmaker, particularly if they have been funding the nonprofit for a while. Generally the endowment principal is held as a long-term investment for the organization, and the interest income is used each year for operating needs.

Definitions

Earned Income. "Money received by an organization in return for the sale of a product or rendered service."

Capacity Building. "The development of an organization's core skills and capabilities, such as leadership, management, finance and fundraising, programs, and evaluation, in order to build the organization's effectiveness and sustainability."

The Proposal Process

In truth there is no magic to writing a successful proposal. The keys to success are

- Developing a clear plan for your program (or operations growth or capital work)
- Researching funders thoroughly
- Building strong relationships with funders
- Targeting your proposals carefully
- Writing a concise proposal

Whether you are preparing a proposal for a foundation or a corporation, the process of proposal writing will be essentially the same. You will

- Identify an unmet need that your organization can or should address.
- Develop your plan to meet the need.
- Identify potential funders and begin to build relationships with them.
- Write the proposals, with each being tailored specifically for one potential funder.
- Engage in strategic follow-up once the proposal has been submitted.

This book covers the proposal process in detail in Steps One through Twelve. The major components of a proposal are as follows:

- *Cover letter:* a short letter that accompanies the proposal and briefly describes its significance
- *Executive summary* (or *proposal summary* or *summary):* a very brief (usually one to two pages) overview of the proposal
- *Need statement* (or *statement of need* or *problem statement):* a compelling description of the need to be addressed by the applicant organization
- *Goals and objectives:* a description of what the organization ultimately hopes to accomplish with a project (goal), and a spelling out of the specific results or outcomes to be accomplished (objectives)
- *Methods* (or *strategies):* a description of the programs, services, and activities that will achieve the desired results
- *Evaluation:* a plan for assessing program accomplishments
- *Sustainability:* a presentation of the nonprofit's strategies for developing additional funding to continue the program after the initial grant funding is over

- *Organization background* (or *background statement*): a presentation of the nonprofit's qualifications to carry out the proposed project (try keeping this to two to three pages maximum)
- *Budget:* a line-item summary of program revenues and expenses

Your proposal's format and length will vary depending on the grant-maker. In general, proposals contain the same key components to help funders understand that your organization has a sound plan that meets an important need and will make a positive impact on whomever it serves. The format laid out in this book is commonly used among funders but is by no means the only format possible. The step-by-step process here is a useful and hands-on way to develop your thoughts and present your project. After you follow these well-defined steps, it will be easy for you to put your results into whatever order the funder requests. *The importance of following each grantmaker's guidelines cannot be emphasized enough.* These guidelines will walk you through each funder's requirements for proposal development, packaging, and submission. The proposals on the CD included with this workbook show some of the different formats required by different funders. Many foundations belong to a regional association of grantmakers (RAG); RAGs provide education, networking, and services to their members, and advocate for foundations' interests and concerns with policymakers. Members of a RAG may use a common statewide or regional application form (a form used in the Washington, D.C., area is shown on the CD; see file titled Washington Grantmakers' Common Grant Application), which makes the process of grantseeking easier. Be sure to check with your local RAG to find out if common applications exist in your area.

Types of Proposals

Broadly speaking, there are three types of proposals.

A *letter of intent* (or *letter of inquiry*) is generally a two- or three-page summary (though some funders may request a specific number of pages) submitted when the funder wishes to see a brief description of the project before deciding whether to ask for a longer, more detailed proposal. This document must focus on how the proposed project fits the priorities of the funder. It should also clearly describe the need and outline the plan to meet it.

A *letter proposal* is the type most often requested by corporations. It is typically a three- or four-page description of the project plan, the organization requesting the funds, and the actual request. The letter proposal and the letter of intent are often confused by grantseekers. In the letter proposal you are actually requesting funds. In the letter of intent you are only introducing your idea to the funder in order to determine whether the funder has an interest in receiving a more detailed proposal.

The *long proposal* (or *full proposal*), a format that includes a cover letter and a proposal summary, is the type most often requested by foundations. Corporations should not receive this format unless they specifically request it. Long proposals range from five to twenty-five pages, with most funders being interested in receiving about seven to ten pages, plus attachments. In the longer proposal, the grantseeker has an opportunity to give many details about the project and its importance to the community. When using this longer format, you should make sure that the funding request—the actual dollar amount—is not hidden. It should appear in the cover letter and in the summary as well as in the body of the proposal.

In some instances, funders—mostly the larger grantmaking institutions—are now requiring grantseekers to fill out applications in the form of online templates. (See the Reality Check box on page 25 in Step Two for more information about this process.)

Tips for Writing Proposals

Don't let grantwriters write the proposal! The most articulate, passionate, and knowledgeable communicator about your project is the person who has conceived it. This is usually not a grantwriter; it is the program person who will run it. Grantwriters may be able to provide the bones for an application, but they cannot add the "intangibles" that jump off the page when you are reviewing a proposal.

GWEN I. WALDEN
Principal, Walden Philanthropy Advisors
Former Director, The Center for Healthy Communities
The California Endowment (a private statewide foundation)

The three key things I would advise organizations to keep in mind when writing proposals are

- Imagine the reader as you write. I've always liked to picture the reader as a friendly, well-educated aunt—she hasn't seen you in a while, and doesn't know exactly what you do, but she's interested. What would you tell her to share your excitement and sense of mission?

- Find the right mix of facts and stories. Foundations vary in what they seek in terms of the right mix of vignettes and numbers. The aim is to show them why and how your approach to a problem they care about will get great results and will offer them the best return on their investment.

- It's not just a grant, it's an investment. Foundations have limited resources, and want to show their board and the larger community that they've put their money where it will make a difference, to advance the foundation's mission. Just like investors in stocks and funds, foundation investors will vary in their appetite for risk (a new organization, an untried approach), and balance that against perceived returns (lives saved, children educated, workers back on the job, etc.).

SUSAN G. ZEPEDA, PhD
Executive Director
Foundation for a Healthy Kentucky

The heart and soul of your organization's proposal will come from those who have identified the need and conceptualized the program to address it; they must be an integral part of the proposal development process. You need to decide on one person to write the proposal—either the staff person with the strongest writing skills or an outside grantwriter—and have that person "joined at the hip" with those who developed the program to be funded. Keep in mind that the proposal will suffer if the writer selected—whether internal staff or outside grantwriter—does not have an understanding of what the project is, why it is important to the community, and why the organization seeking funding is best qualified to undertake the project. And even when the writer does have this understanding, it is essential to have the program staff involved in the development of the grant proposal.

Stick to the following principles when preparing the proposal:

- *Follow the grant guidelines.* You do not want your organization's proposal dismissed on a technicality, which happens more than most grantseekers think. It is common for grantmakers to make explicit the format they want followed. Make the proposal visually attractive, but do not overdo it. Whenever possible, break up the written page. Use a reasonable font size, and use bulleted lists and other formatting tools to make each page look inviting—but follow the instructions outlined by each individual funder.

- *Get the facts straight.* Make sure you have relevant and up-to-date data to support the need for your project. You want enough general data to help you set a framework for the statement of need, but the most important data are the facts and figures specific to the geographical area served, target audience, and other key elements.

- *Do not assume that it is "always darkest before the dawn" when it comes to grant proposals.* Do not make your organization's proposal so bleak that the reader sees no point in trying to address the need. Use a positive writing style, but present a well-reasoned, thoughtful presentation. A grant proposal should contain some elements of emotional appeal yet also be realistic and factual.

- *Be aware that many program officers read the executive summary first, followed closely by the program budget.* If they go beyond your executive summary and budget—*congratulations;* you have at a minimum sparked their interest. For this reason you should consider developing the proposal summary last.

- *KISS (Keep It Sweet and Simple).* Avoid jargon and do not overwrite. Make it easy for someone who probably is not an expert in your particular field to read, understand, and successfully digest the entire proposal. Jargon (specialized words that only people in the relevant field will understand) acts as a barrier to understanding, and people cannot be sympathetic to things they cannot comprehend. Be thrifty with your words, but do not sacrifice information that is critical to making the case for the project.

- *Get some honest feedback on your proposal before you send it to a funder.* Ask one or two people (maybe a staff or board member or even someone outside your organization) to review the proposal carefully. Does everything make sense? Is the need clear? Do the proposed objectives (Step Four) and methods (Step Five) seem to be an appropriate response to the need? Use the answers to these questions to strengthen the final proposal.

- *Remember that one size does* not *fit all.* After you have developed a proposal, study the guidelines of each prospective funder you have identified as a possible match for your program and tailor the proposal for each one accordingly. It is true that most grantmakers want the same basic information. That said, it is also true that they request it in different formats, which will require reordering sections, cutting and pasting, and possibly relabeling some sections (for instance, the need statement may become the problem statement). Occasionally, you will have to add material to or delete it from your original version. By tailoring your proposal for each grantmaker, you will be giving each proposal reviewer confidence that the proposal is responding to the specific funder's concerns.

- *Plan ahead.* The grantseeking process typically operates within six- to nine-month windows, and each funder operates on its own schedule. From the time you submit a proposal to the time you hear back from the funder will be on average six months, and many funders have specific deadlines for receiving proposals. Develop a calendar that lists all your foundation and corporation prospects and their deadlines. Also maintain a list of each funder's priorities that seem applicable to the proposal you want to develop for that funder, and then be sure to clearly spell out the parts of your organization's program that fit those priorities. This calendar will help you stay organized and on track as you juggle numerous deadline dates and priority areas.

Step 1

Developing the Proposal Idea

I often have people call or e-mail me asking if they can tell me about their work and apply for a grant. If I know the work is not a fit at all, I'm honest. It's important to hear when a funder is telling you this. Even if *you* think you are a perfect fit, you may not be. Trying to coax a funder into thinking you are can oftentimes backfire.

—DESIREE FLORES
Program Officer, Health
Ms. Foundation for Women (a national operating
foundation in New York City)

NOW THAT YOU have had an introduction to the process of preparing a proposal, let's take that first step! This section of the workbook will walk you through developing your proposal idea by answering some key questions. Before you can begin writing a proposal, you must first determine which projects in your organization are the most "fundable." That is, which programs are most likely to be attractive to grantmakers as an investment and are in need of funding? Most funders have a fairly strong preference for investing in new and expanding programs over general operating support or basic program continuation. Again, be sure to do a thorough job of researching your prospective funders (refer to Resource B) so that you are clear on the audience with which you have to work. Funders might also have an interest in a special project, such as a new time-specific project, a capacity-building idea, a set of technology improvements, or technical assistance. However, because general funder preference is for new and expanding programs, this workbook uses the idea of launching a new program as the model for developing a proposal.

To start developing your proposal idea, begin with the end in mind. Your organization has identified an unmet need, which is why it wants to develop a program to address that need. So sit down with everyone

Helpful Hint

General operating support. Take note: some funders are currently displaying a slow but growing interest in general operating and ongoing program support, so the CD that accompanies this workbook includes a sample funded proposal to help grantseekers in approaching sources for these funds as well.

involved to begin to flesh out this program idea—how your organization is going to meet that unmet need it has identified. Use a team approach in developing the plan and involve the appropriate staff, clients, and volunteers *from the very beginning.* Your team can develop an initial program plan first, which then will become the basis of the entire proposal. The importance of having the right people at the table when the program plan is developed cannot be emphasized enough. One of the worst things that can happen to a nonprofit is to be funded for a program that it then discovers it does not have the ability to successfully implement or, worse yet, a program that does *not* effectively meet the needs initially identified because it was developed in a vacuum—or in the development director's office—rather than with the individuals who will be responsible for implementing it. In addition, securing grant funding usually means a change will take place within the organization. That means another important reason to involve people in the organization with the planning is so they will be more enthusiastic about implementing the change.

When preparing a proposal, many writers start with the planning sections (need statement, objectives, methods, evaluation, program sustainability, and budget) because these sections form the core of the proposal. Then they write the organization background section, finishing with the summary and the cover letter. This workbook follows that format.

The planning sections of the proposal deserve careful attention; without a clearly articulated program plan, it is nearly impossible to get funding. (Refer to number two of the top five grantseeking mistakes, outlined in the Introduction.) As one funder we talked to told us, "Writing a clear, goal-oriented, thoughtful proposal is crucial. If you can't explain what you're doing, why you're doing it, how you're going to do it, in a way that is easily understandable, no program officer in the world will be able to advocate for you."

A guideline here is that nonprofits should expect to focus approximately 80 percent of their time on program planning; the other 20 percent can be dedicated to writing and packaging the proposal. Also, the "tighter" your program plan, the easier the proposal will be to write. Go into this process knowing that even with all of your planning, you will be fine-tuning your plan as the proposal is being developed—this is common practice.

Logic Models in Program Design

What exactly is a *logic model?* In a nutshell, a logic model is a valuable tool that produces a basic program "picture" that shows how the organization's program is intended to work. The tool also helps you outline the sequence of related events in your program. These events provide a direct and visual connection between the need for the planned program and the desired results and outcomes expected from the program. A logic model can be particularly useful when it comes to designing the evaluation for your new program. Funders are beginning to use logic modeling more and more as the competition for their limited grant funding continues to grow. (Some funders use terms such as *theory of change* to describe this type of analysis; for example, you will hear a funder speak of theory of change in Step Two of this book. For other funders these ideas are distinct.) The W. K. Kellogg Foundation has an excellent free publication, the *Logic Model Development Guide,* that provides numerous examples of types and styles of logic models. Several funders participating in this workbook indicated that they direct their potential grantees to this resource as a reference. (To view this guide, go to http://www.wkkf.org/Pubs/Tools/Evaluation/Pub3669.pdf.) In addition, Resource C in this workbook displays an example of a basic logic model taken from the Kellogg guide.

Reality Check

Check the fit. When conducting prospect research, you will come across many wonderful opportunities presented by grantmakers—special initiatives, and pots of funding for specific programs and projects within defined fields of interest. And even though they might sound exciting and worthwhile, always measure every funding opportunity by your organization's mission. Is there really a fit—a natural, organic fit? Or is your organization "growing another foot" to fit the "shoe" the funder has to offer? Always, always use your organization's mission and organizational purpose as your guide.

To get started on developing a fundable proposal idea, complete Worksheet 1.1. The more thorough you can be with your answers, the more helpful the worksheet will be to you. After answering the questions in Worksheet 1.1 use those answers to identify one specific idea to develop using the exercises in this book. To check the merit of the idea you have identified, ask the Proposal Development Review Questions at the end of this step. Then follow Steps Two through Twelve to create your own, well-planned proposal. Throughout these steps, this workbook will provide examples and worksheets to assist you.

WORKSHEET 1.1:
Proposal Idea Questionnaire

1. **What new projects is your organization planning for the next two to three years?**

   Project A:

   Project B:

   Project C:

   Project D:

2. **Which of these projects are most compatible with your organization's current mission and purpose, and in what way?**

Project	Compatibility
A	
B	
C	
D	

3. **What is unique about your organization's project?**

Project	Uniqueness
A	
B	
C	
D	

4. **Who else is doing this project? Is there duplication of effort? Is there potential for collaboration?**

Project	Duplicate Project (with whom)	Possible Collaboration (with whom)
A		
B		
C		
D		

5. **What community need does each of your organization's projects address?**

   Project   Need Addressed

   A

   B

   C

   D

6. **What members of your community—including civic leaders, political figures, the media, your organization's clients or constituents, and other nonprofits—support each project?**

   Project   Supporters

   A

   B

   C

   D

7. **Does your organization currently have the expertise to undertake each project? If new staff are necessary, can the organization manage growth in infrastructure (HR, technology, supervisory oversight, and so forth) effectively? (Check each category that applies to each project.)**

Project	Expertise	HR	Technology	Other (specify)
A				
B				
C				
D				

8. **Is there internal (board and staff) support for the project? External support (community leaders, clients, neighbors, and so forth)? (Check the category that applies to each project and specify the type of support.)**

Project	Internal Support (specify)	External Support (specify)
A		
B		
C		
D		

Proposal Development Review Questions

To find out whether the proposal idea you have developed has merit, answer the following six questions:

1. What community need does the program or service your organization has identified address? (The answer to this question will become the basis of your proposal's *need statement*.)

2. What would an improved community situation look like? (This answer will become the basis of your proposal's *goals and objectives*.)

3. What can your organization do to improve this situation? (This answer will become the basis of your proposal's *methods*.)

4. How will you know if your organization's program or service has succeeded? (This answer will become the basis of your proposal's program *evaluation*.)

5. How much will your organization's program or service cost, and what other sources of funding will it have? (This answer will become the basis of your proposal's program *budget*.)

6. How will your organization's program or service be funded in the future? (This answer will become the basis of your proposal's program *sustainability*.)

Now that you have successfully identified your organization's proposal idea, let's move on to Step Two, which will address a critical part of winning grants: developing relationships with funders.

Developing Relationships with Funders

I think it is really important to develop a relationship over time. Finding shared values is what we look for so that we know we can work together in the long term. So, my advice is, don't try to be something you're not. Be yourself, date us for awhile and see if we can make our relationship work.

To me, chasing the money is inappropriate. In other words, doing or creating something just to get a grant. The best approach is always honest, open communication. We may not fund you, but we might in the future or recommend you to someone else.

—VALERIE JACOBS HAPKE
Board Member
Jacobs Family Foundation (in San Diego, California)

DO YOU KNOW anyone who has run a marathon? Did she wake up one day and decide to run a marathon, go out and purchase running gear, register for the marathon, and then simply show up on the day of the event and run 26.5 miles? Or did she instead get cleared by her doctor, change her diet, and begin a rigorous training program over a number of months that slowly built up her physical and mental ability to successfully complete the marathon?

Developing relationships with funders is a marathon, not a sprint. It takes a diligent, strategic approach over a period of time if it is ultimately to be successful. Once you have determined that your organization's proposed program is solid, you need to put some time and focused effort into identifying funders who are a match with what you propose to do. Resource B offers some tips on how to conduct your research to successfully identify possible funders for your program. Step Two also provides you with no-nonsense advice about this research and then offers ideas for developing relationships once funders are identified—some of this advice comes directly from the funders themselves. Program and other officers with various types of foundations have contributed their thoughts to this particular step, which we hope will contribute greatly to your understanding of how you can—and should—initially approach prospective funders and develop a relationship with them *prior* to submitting a proposal.

Making the Initial Approach

These days you will typically find an abundance of information on a grantmaker's website: background information on the foundation as an institution, its staff and board of directors, grant guidelines, and special funding initiatives, if any. You are also likely to find successful grant stories and lists of organizations or programs the foundation has funded in the past—the best indicator of what it is likely to fund in the future. Some funders may have additional separate websites for particular funding initiatives they have launched. That said, other funders may still require additional "sleuthing" on your part before you can glean whether there is truly a match. So in addition to reviewing funder websites, visit GuideStar (www.guidestar.org) to review the most recent Internal Revenue Service Form 990 filed by the grantmakers you are vetting, use Google and other search engines to research their previous giving to other organizations and perhaps also to look for feature stories about them (if not found on their websites), or pick up the telephone and call a foundation directly. But be prepared: this conversation just might lead to a brief discussion of your proposed project or program, so be ready to talk about it and hit the highlights. Who knows? This may be the start of a great new relationship. After you have reviewed a grantmaker's website and other related materials, you need to be clear that there is a potentially solid *fit* between your organization's proposed program or project and what the grantmaker says it is interested in funding. Take a look at what one grantmaker has to say about this subject:

> Recognize that the relationship you make with Foundation staff is one based on mutual need, and be on a mission to educate foundation staff on what they need from your organization. A foundation will need to find organizations whose work will demonstrate their particular theory of change or point of view about what it takes to bring about lasting positive results—i.e. results from after school programs or from youth violence prevention efforts. Do your homework. Minimize your turn-downs

by not approaching a foundation until you are clear about what their hunches are about what works and what doesn't, and how your organization can help them to act successfully on those hunches. This will give you real advantage in building a relationship that ends in sustained funding.

—SANDRA BROCK JIBRELL
Former Director of Civic Investments
Annie E. Casey Foundation (a national private
foundation in Baltimore, Maryland)

Definition

Theory of Change. "A Theory of Change defines all building blocks required to bring about a given long-term goal" (this definition is from ActKnowledge and the Aspen Institute Roundtable on Community Change [www.theoryofchange.org]).

Do not assume that funders know and understand your organization's mission or target audience or that the program you are presenting is addressing a priority of theirs. More times than not, grantseekers do not take enough time up front to define the idea in a way that makes the grantmaker see the fit between the grantseeker's need and the grantmaker's priorities as an institution.

Developing the Relationship

After you establish that there is a good fit, then the relationship building becomes a continuous process that begins before you write the proposal and spans many years—yes, years! Good communication with your funders should never end, even though you may stop receiving grants from them. Once a relationship exists, funders like to receive progress reports about how the organization or program they funded is doing. They may also take an interest in other fundable ideas that your organization has developed. See what other grantmakers have to say about this:

It's not always easy to develop relationships with funders, especially if they have not funded your organization previously. However, the key is the *relationship* part of that phrase. It's relationship building, rather than selling, that makes a difference.

If you are totally unfamiliar with the person and/or foundation, try to make an appointment or set up a phone call—promise a short one and keep that promise. Then use the opportunity to describe your organization and its activities, and ask about the funding entity and its priorities. If there's no fit, don't force-fit. Funders usually catch on to that pretty quickly. By the way, this is not (or should not be) an adversarial process—grantmakers and grantseekers generally are trying to achieve the same things, it's just that one has the financial resources, and the other has or should have the other resources needed to achieve positive results.

—EDWARD B. KACIC, MBA, CAIA
President & CEO
Irvine Health Foundation (a regional private
foundation in Orange County, California)

Organizations should realize that the majority of funders are much more interested in a meaningful and engaged relationship that is beyond the simple grant transaction. This type of relationship is built over time and requires a commitment to actively listen to each other in an active, mutual learning posture. My most enduring relationships with grantees have been with the ones from whom I have learned the most, and who took the time to inform and educate me about their core business. This type of relationship requires a deep level of trust and honesty between funder and applicant organizations or grantees. My best experiences have been when each of us has been willing to take the risk of telling each other the truth.

—GWEN I. WALDEN
Principal, Walden Philanthropy Advisors
Former Director, The Center for Healthy Communities
The California Endowment (a private statewide foundation)

Here are a few concrete ways to approach a funder to open the door to relationship building. They are discussed more fully in the following subsections.

- Send the funder a brief e-mail inquiry.
- Call the foundation, and speak with someone regarding your proposal idea.

- Send a letter of inquiry to the funder.

- Have meetings with the funder.

While grant guidelines determine a nonprofit's initial approach, you may have a connection to the funder, either directly or through one or more contacts who can potentially open a door on your behalf for an initial meeting or phone conversation.

Reality Check

Be strategic and err on the side of restraint when using a contact to open a door for you with a funder. Few things are worse than dealing with a program officer who feels "pushed" into a meeting with you. You always want an invitation, rather than a meeting based on obligation.

Sending E-Mail Inquiries to Funders

Many funders offer grantseekers the option of contacting them via e-mail with questions and funding inquiries. Some grantmakers even provide direct e-mail access to their program officers from their websites; others may have an "info@" e-mail that is routed to the appropriate staff person after review. In either case, e-mail is a valuable tool for stimulating further, more meaningful, contact because it provides you with an opportunity to briefly introduce yourself, your organization, and the program needing funding and at the same time it gives the program officer the time he needs to review your information and respond. E-mail is far less demanding for program officers than a phone call and less wasteful than paper documents. The key is to keep it brief! You can also request an in-person meeting or time for a phone conversation in your e-mail, which then provides the funder with options for communicating with you.

Contacting a Funder by Telephone

Before you telephone a funder to describe your idea, be prepared. The person with whom you speak may have only a short time for a conversation, and you need to be ready to provide the highlights of your organization's program within a ten- to fifteen-minute conversation. This time frame includes the time it may take for the person to ask for clarification of your points. Remember that you are not *selling* your organization's program to a funder; you are attempting to *make a connection* between the program and the funding institution's interest areas. You are also building a long-term relationship with the funder and with this particular representative, so listening carefully to the funder's needs and providing information the funder wants is extremely important.

In listening to the funder's needs, you might discover—sometimes very early in the conversation—that there in fact is not a match between the program your organization is introducing and the funder's current funding priorities; that is why you should have one or two other program ideas in mind to present as a backup. You do not want to waste this opportunity with the funder, so be fully prepared.

Speaking of being prepared, please review the article in Resource D, written by Sarah S. Brophy for CharityChannel's *Grants & Foundations Review.* Published in 2002, it is titled *Making the Call,* and in it Brophy offers sage advice on contacting a funder by telephone.

Writing a Letter of Inquiry

More funders are starting to request a *letter of inquiry* (or LOI) as the first step in their funding process. An LOI provides the funder with a "sneak peek" at your organization, target audience, and prospective program, without requiring the grantseeker to develop a full proposal at this early stage. After the funder has reviewed the information in your organization's LOI, you may or may not be invited to submit a full proposal. Even though an LOI is a preliminary step, you should treat it as a vital part of relationship building. It is an integral first interaction of what you hope to be many interactions with the funder. If you are asked to submit an LOI, check to see if the funder has specific LOI guidelines. If it does not, the following list suggests what information to include, as a general rule:

- Your organization's mission and related programs
- The need your organization wishes to meet
- The outcome you expect from your organization's project
- General details of how your organization will conduct the project
- The fit you see between the funder and your organization

The sample LOI included in this step presents to a funder the Senior Latino Community Outreach Pilot Project, which was introduced earlier and will be used as the example project throughout this workbook. This is the letter the Some City Senior Center would mail (or e-mail, as this is becoming the preferred method of delivery for more and more foundations) if an LOI was invited by the funder or if the funder accepted unsolicited submissions.

Now that you have had an opportunity to review an LOI example, take the time to answer the questions in Worksheet 2.1 as clearly as you can. This

Sample Letter of Inquiry

Mary Smith, PhD
Program Officer
Community Foundation
4321 Common Lane
Some City, YZ 55555

Dear Dr. Smith:

I am pleased to submit this letter of inquiry to the Community Foundation to determine your interest in receiving a full proposal for the Some City Senior Center's Senior Latino Community Outreach Pilot Project. We are respectfully requesting your consideration of a grant in the amount of $50,000.

This project is our first major outreach effort to serve the Latino community of elders—both Spanish and English speaking—with health and social services. We thought you might find our project of particular interest, as it closely aligns with three of the areas you list as current priorities: (1) providing access to health services for seniors in Any County, (2) increasing the outreach to and inclusion of the Spanish-speaking population, specifically in Valley Vista, and (3) increasing local service organizations' overall cultural competence.

The Some City Senior Center was established in 1994. We are the largest senior center in Any County, and we have a 92% approval rating from our members as of our February 2008 member satisfaction survey. Our center's mission is to help seniors improve and maintain a healthy and independent lifestyle and to maximize their quality of life. More than 450 older adults are served each day by participating in the many programs and services offered at the Some City Senior Center.

Any County has a rapidly growing older adult population. In the four-city area we serve, this population has more than doubled since 1990 and is expected to double again over the next two decades. In Any County, 37% of Spanish-speaking older adults reported income below the poverty levels in 2007.

Our center serves older adults from Some City and three other cities: Valley Vista, Grove Beach, and Hill Viejo. Two of these cities (Valley Vista and Hill Viejo) along with Some City have the highest concentrations of low-income minority older adults in Any County. Of these cities, Valley Vista has the largest Latino population: approximately 70%, and of that Latino group, more than 50% are monolingual Spanish speaking.

We currently have the capacity to significantly increase—by at least 25 to 30%—the number of clients served by our center by expanding our programs and services to effectively accommodate and incorporate Spanish language offerings. Our board of directors is eager and enthusiastic to launch this program in an effort to be the most inclusive, responsive, and culturally competent center for seniors in all of the communities we propose to serve.

Our center will serve as a primary referral for Health Access Latinos, Families of Any County, and three community clinics within a fifteen-mile radius of the center. Our program objectives include (1) increasing by 50% the number of monolingual Spanish-speaking seniors who access the services of our center for the first time, (2) engaging a minimum of 50 Latino seniors in our new healthy Mexican food cooking class, and (3) increasing our referrals of Latino seniors from the community clinics and partnering nonprofit organizations specifically serving the Latino community by 50% within the grant period.

The total cost of implementation of our Senior Latino Community Outreach Pilot Project is $190,000. Of this amount, $140,000 has already been committed from both the county government and other funders. Your investment of $50,000 will complete the funding we need to fully implement this pilot project, and we are excited about the prospect of partnering with you. If you have any questions or would like to receive a full proposal, please feel free to contact me at (555) 555-5555. We deeply appreciate your consideration of our request and look forward to hearing from you soon.

Sincerely,
Jane Lovely
Executive Director

exercise will help you develop a strong letter of inquiry for funders. If you find you cannot clearly and articulately answer the questions, that probably means that you need to gather more information before you can effectively complete an LOI.

Meeting with a Funder

Many grantseekers dream of having face-to-face meetings with prospective funders prior to submitting a proposal because they want to get not only clarification from the funders on key issues but also an opportunity to "prime the pump" and get the grantmakers excited about the program even before they receive the proposal. Unfortunately, preproposal funder meetings are few and far between, because funders simply cannot accommodate every nonprofit's request for them. Additionally, some funders are leery of these meetings because they do not want to raise unrealistic funding expectations in grantseekers. Managing grantseeker expectations is of the utmost importance to the vast majority of funders: they certainly want to encourage the submission of proposals for programs meeting their interest areas, but they do not want to raise false hope at the same time. Remember, every foundation and corporate grantmaker has a limited amount of funding available for grants every year. That said, if you know someone who already has a strong relationship with a funder, this individual may be able to help you set up a meeting. After doing your funder research, think about whom you know who may also know your organization's prospective funders. Understand also that any early meeting you may get with the grantmaker will be very preliminary and in no way ensures that your nonprofit will receive funds from this source.

If you are successful in scheduling an in-person meeting, take materials that best describe your organization and the proposed program. In your meeting you should cover the following topics:

- Credibility of the organization
- Program description, need for the proposed project
- Community interest in the program, proposed outcomes
- Your ability to measure its success
- Costs and projected revenue sources
- Why you believe this funder's interests may be met by investing in the project

Your time with the funder's program officer will likely be short, so be prepared to hit the highlights. Listen carefully to the funder's questions and any concerns expressed, and make sure you answer them fully and truthfully. These questions and concerns should also be addressed again in the proposal that you will mail after your meeting, assuming you have found a good fit—so be alert and take good notes on the questions asked and on the general tone and direction of the conversation.

Here are some additional steps to take to develop good relationships with funders with whom you have talked:

- Add the program officer to your organization's mailing list or list serve.

- Add the program officer to your organization's newsletter distribution list, and go the extra distance by including a personal note with his newsletter.

- Send brief (one- to two-page) progress reports on the successes of your organization's other programs—ones that the program officer has not funded but that his colleagues at other foundations and corporations have.

- Invite the program officer to your organization's events with personal notes—even if she cannot come, she will remember the contact.

- Contact the program officer occasionally by telephone or e-mail with brief messages and updates. Include quotes or even notes specifically from program constituents.

Developing relationships with funders is such an important step in the process of winning grants that the value of doing it well cannot be emphasized enough. Now we are moving into the nuts-and-bolts section of your proposal, starting with the development of your needs statement.

Reality Check

Electronic applications. Over the last few years there has been a slow-building movement by some foundations to use online grant applications. These are web-based forms for grantseekers to fill in. They have a space for each proposal component, and they limit the number of words that you can use per space. Some funders use these tools as application cover forms to accompany paper grant proposals, whereas others use these online templates as substitutes for paper grant proposals. When you must use a funder's online application as the grant proposal, you are likely to find developing a relationship with that funder even more challenging than such relationship building is ordinarily. Among the funders using electronic applications are the W. K. Kellogg Foundation (www.wkkf.org), Ford Foundation (www.fordfoundation.org), The Skoll Foundation (www.skollfoundation.org), and The Humana Foundation (www.humanafoundation.org). Please visit any one of these foundation websites to see clear examples of online application processes.

WORKSHEET 2.1:
Letter of Inquiry Questionnaire

1. What is the purpose of this letter of inquiry? To whom is it being sent, and what is the connection?

2. What year was your organization founded? What year was it incorporated?

3. What is the mission of your organization?

4. What are the long-term goals for your organization?

5. What programs does your organization provide that support these goals?

6. What is the need in your community that you seek funding to address?

7. How, in your organization's view, is the need related to its programs, long-term goals, and mission?

8. What does your organization propose to do about this need?

9. What outcome does your organization anticipate after the first year of funding?

10. What is the total cost of the proposed idea for the first year (or multiple years if you plan to request multiple-year funding)? How much do you want from this funder?

11. Who will be contacting the funder to determine its interest and when? Whom should the funder contact for more information?

Now that you have finished answering the questions, you can use the resulting information to build a solid letter of inquiry. The ideal way to write the letter is to follow this format: opening, background, problem statement, proposed solution, closing. The questions you answered here followed this format.

Letter of Inquiry Review Questions

1. Do you clearly state the name of your project and amount of your request in the first paragraph?

2. Does your second paragraph elaborate further on your proposed project, as well as any related projects (when applicable)?

3. Is your mission statement included?

4. Have you clearly stated the need your proposed program intends to meet? Do you provide some preliminary data to support the need for your proposed project?

5. Have you articulated the specific outcomes your project is targeted to achieve?

6. Do you include how your organization will go about implementing the project?

7. Do you highlight the "fit" or natural connection between your organization's project and the funder's priority areas, as identified in their guidelines?

8. If there is some funding already committed to the project, do you mention it in the LOI?

9. Do you clearly indicate who the contact person is at your organization and provide all relevant contact information?

Step 3

Writing a Compelling Need Statement

IN THIS STEP you will learn the key elements of a need statement, including the four requirements for it to be successful. Then a worksheet and sample will guide you in preparing a statement of need for your organization's proposal.

Purpose of the Need Statement

What is the need to be addressed? Your organization's need statement will—or at least it should—directly address this question. Therefore this is the best place to begin writing your proposal. A need statement sets the framework for the entire proposal, as it describes a critical condition, set of conditions, or a social need affecting certain people or things in a specific place at a specific time. The need statement is fundamental to your proposal because funders must agree with the organization that the project meets an important need. Bolstered by accurate data (quantitative statistics) combined with the right selection of stories that provide a more personal illustration of the need (qualitative data), a compelling need statement is often the component that motivates a funder to give serious consideration to a nonprofit's request. Make no mistake: a good, solid, and well-supported need statement is the key that unlocks the door, moving your proposal that much closer to funding consideration.

Finally, the need—and your organization's ability to successfully address it—gives grantmakers an opportunity to realize their own goals.

Content of the Need Statement

Here are some basic rules to follow when developing the project's needs statement:

- The need you address in the statement should have a clear relationship to your organization's mission and purpose.

- The need statement should focus squarely on those the organization serves and their specific needs, rather than your organization's needs—unless you are specifically seeking a capacity-building grant.

- Any assertions about the need should be well supported with evidence (statistical facts, expert views, trends found in the experience of doing the work, and so on).

- You must be able to directly connect—and substantiate—the need you describe in the proposal with your organization's ability to successfully respond to that need (that ability will be described in a subsequent section of the proposal).

- The need statement must be easily digestible. You accomplish this by KISSing (Keeping It Sweet and Simple). Avoid using jargon, and do not make the reader have to work to understand what you are trying to say.

The need your organization is addressing may be specific to its geographical area or it may be found in many communities. Be careful not to overpromise: if the need occurs in an area larger than that served by your organization, it is important to focus only on what your organization can reasonably accomplish. That said, if this is your nonprofit's situation, consider positioning your organization's program as a potential model for other nonprofts in other locations. By taking the model approach, an organization broadens the pool of potential funders to include those concerned with the need in other geographical areas. You might also want to research to find out if other organizations in your service area have—or are developing—similar programs to address the same need. Should this be the case, consider exploring a collaborative program that would leverage and expand the reach of your plans and grant funds.

If your organization decides to take either the model or collaborative approach, make mention in the need statement that your organization is addressing the need on a larger level through the development of a program that can be a model for others or that it is leveraging its efforts with another organization so it can expand the reach and impact of its program. Then in the methods component (discussed in Step Five), you should discuss how the

---

Definition

Collaboration. "A mutually beneficial and well-defined relationship entered into by two or more organizations to achieve common goals. The relationship includes a commitment to mutual relationships and goals, a jointly developed structure and shared responsibility, mutual authority and accountability for success, and sharing of resources and rewards."

program information will be disseminated to other organizations or exactly how the collaborative process will work with the partnering organization(s).

Oftentimes arts organizations struggle with this section owing to a perception that the arts do not meet a compelling community need. However, if you represent an arts organization, be encouraged. Arts organizations do meet important needs. Without these nonprofits, certain cultures and traditions would be lost, lives would not be enriched, and young people would not learn new and different ways of expressing themselves. Additionally, with national media efforts such as VH-1's Save-the-Music (http://www.vh1.com/partners/save_the_music) as examples, you will be able to find even more substantive statistics as well as qualitative data than you could before to support the statement that the arts have been proven to significantly enhance the learning process for both children and adults.

The same holds true for nonprofits seeking general support grants. You might struggle with the statement of need because your proposal addresses the general work of the organization. Focus on describing the needs the organization meets: mission and purpose. This, again, goes back to something touched on earlier in this workbook: when focusing on soliciting general operating support, always use your nonprofit's mission and purpose as your guide.

Tips for Writing the Need Statement

As impossible as this sounds, try to contain your needs statement within no more than two to three pages—that is, be concise. (Most foundation guidelines limit proposals to ten to twelve pages in total; corporate guidelines typically limit proposals to even fewer pages.)

In stating the need use hard statistics from reputable sources, and steer clear of assumptions and undocumented assertions masquerading as legitimate facts.

- *Use statistics that are clear and that support your argument.* If you are talking about a specific community within a city, you might offer one or two data points about the city, then zero in on the data specific to that community.

- *Use comparative statistics and research where possible.* Look at the examples in the accompanying Reality Check box. As shown, using data from a community that did something very similar to what you want to do and citing the benefits that community derived can make a strong case for the nonprofit to do the same.

- *Quote authorities who have spoken on your topic.* Be sure to cite the person who made each statement and the source where you found it, and if appropriate, provide backup information that substantiates that this person is indeed an authority on the subject matter.

- *Make sure all data collection is well documented.* Most likely you will have used the Internet for your research, which is appropriate. However, make sure that the websites you are referencing are reputable and your links are current; then you need to clearly cite your sources—including those found on the Internet.

- *Use touching stories of people as examples.* This is very effective, but only when balanced against hard data. As one funder interviewed for this workbook stated: "Foundations vary in what they seek in terms of the right mix of vignettes and numbers. That said I haven't met a funder yet who doesn't respond to that one great personal story in a well-supported needs statement that brings the entire proposal to life. Just don't overdo it!"

- *Give a clear sense of the urgency of your request.* Funders need to understand why the funding is important now.

Take a look at the following Sample Need Statement from the Senior Latino Community Outreach Pilot Project. Then, using the proposal idea you identified and developed in Step One, answer the questions on Worksheet 3.1A, as this will assist you as you begin to define the need your organization is addressing. Worksheet 3.1B is an example of a completed questionnaire for the Senior Latino Community Outreach Pilot Project. After reviewing the Sample Need Statement and completing the worksheet questionnaire, write your own organization's statement of need, based on the information you have developed. Next answer the Need Statement Review Questions listed at the end of this step to make sure you have written your statement well. Rewrite your need statement until you feel you have addressed all the review questions.

Reality Check

Avoid the trap of circular reasoning, which commonly occurs in need statements. To use the Foundation Center's definition and example, circular reasoning occurs when "you present the absence of your solution as the actual problem. Then your solution is offered as the way to solve the problem. For example, 'The problem is that we have no pool in our community. Building a pool will solve the problem.'"

This statement does not communicate a problem: communities across the country thrive with no community pool. However, if you stated that a community pool in your neighborhood would specifically address certain challenges your community is facing, and if you followed that up by citing a community similar to yours where a community pool has had a positive impact in ways that are documented, you could potentially build a compelling argument.

Sample Need Statement

According to the 2000 Census, Any County now has the second largest population of our state, with That County being first. Of the approximately 750,000 people in Any County, 114,000 are older adults—or 15.2% of the total population. The number of older adults in Any County increased 21.7% between 1995 and 2005, a greater increase than occurred at the state and national levels.

The Some City Senior Center plays a vital role in the lives of senior residents in the cities of Some City, Valley Vista, Grove Beach, and Hill Viejo. These four cities account for 39.8% of Any County's total senior population. Our four-city service area has a rapidly growing older adult population (people aged 60 and older), which has nearly doubled since 2000 and is expected to double again over the next two decades, as is stated in the Any County's Aging Task Force 2003 report (www.anycounty.gov/agingtf/report/pdf). This same report also asserts that the large numbers of seniors living in Some City, Valley Vista, Grove Beach, and Hill Viejo are largely attributable to the lower rents in those areas compared to the rest of Any County.

Given the demographics of our center's service area, one might assume that a plethora of services would be available to seniors. And while there are some very good fee-for-service and for-profit services available for seniors, the lower rents mentioned in the previous paragraph indicate the socioeconomic reality of many of the seniors in the Some City Senior Center service area. Over 50% of the seniors living in one of the four service cities we serve reported income below the poverty levels according to a survey conducted by the Interagency Committee on Aging (ICG) in 2003. Latino seniors make up nearly 35% of that low-income group, and roughly 20% of these Latino seniors are thought to be monolingual Spanish speakers.

In a survey conducted by the Any County Long-Term Care Multilingual Senior Needs Assessment of 2005, only 3.9% of Spanish-speaking older adults surveyed in our four-city service area reported using senior centers regularly during the previous year, as opposed to 58% of Caucasian seniors. Almost 90% of Spanish-speaking older adults surveyed indicated that they depend primarily on their spouse or other family members for assistance. The survey also indicated that 72.8% of the surveyed individuals reported that they are not at all familiar with any services for older adults—whether with fees or without—which clearly indicates the extent to which this population of seniors is currently being overlooked for health and social services in Any County. The follow-up question in the survey asked about seniors' interest in both learning about and accessing services; nearly 55% indicated that they would be very interested in accessing health, social, and recreational services for seniors—as long as language was not a barrier and/or they felt welcomed.

The board and staff of the Some City Senior Center are fully committed to successfully reaching out to and serving the Latino seniors of Some City, Valley Vista, Grove Beach, and Hill Viejo in order to help them meet their need for health, social, and recreational services—as well as learning and growing in our own cultural competence as an organization dedicated to helping all seniors improve and maintain a healthy and independent lifestyle and maximize their quality of life. We are the largest senior center in Any County and have a 92% satisfaction rate with the seniors we currently serve through our on-site daily meal services, recreation and leisure programs, health screenings, disease management, physical activities, and social services (according to our most recent internal member survey, conducted in February 2007).

As an organization we are conscious of the changing demographics in the center's service area and want very much to respond—and respond appropriately—to them to successfully meet the community's needs. We believe that the need for this pilot project is clearly evident.

WORKSHEET 3.1A:
Statement of Need Questionnaire

Worksheet 3.1B contains sample answers to these questions. Please use it as an example as you complete this questionnaire.

Who? Where? When?	What? Why?	Evidence of Problem	Impact If Problem Is Resolved?
Who is in need (people, animals, land, and so forth)?	What is the need?	What evidence do you have to support your claim?	What will occur if the needs are met? What will be different—and how?
Where are they?	Why does this need exist?		How is the need linked to your organization?
When is the need evident?			

WORKSHEET 3.1B:
Statement of Need Questionnaire Example

Who? Where? When?	What? Why?	Evidence of Problem	Impact If Problem Is Resolved?
Who is in need (people, animals, land, and so forth)? • *Senior Latino adults—both bilingual and monolingual.* Where are they? • *Within our service area of Some City, Valley Vista, Grove Beach, and Hill Viejo.*	What is the need? • *No senior services offered in Spanish, resulting in access issues.* • *Healthy and vibrant seniors without access to or knowledge of services that can significantly increase their quality of life.*	What evidence do you have to support your claim? • *Any County has a rapidly growing older adult population; the population in our four-city service area has more than doubled since 1990 and is expected to double again over the next two decades. In Any County, 37% of Spanish-speaking older adults reported income below the poverty level.* • *Our center serves older adults from four cities, three of which have the highest concentrations of low-income, minority, older adults in Any County. Those cities are Valley Vista, Grove Beach, and Hill Viejo. Of these three cities, Valley Vista has the largest Latino population. Its population is approximately 70% Latino, and in that Latino group over 50% are monolingual Spanish speaking.*	What will occur if the needs are met? What will be different—and how? • *A minimum of 75 Spanish-speaking seniors with Type II diabetes who complete our disease management classes will maintain stabilized blood sugar levels for three consecutive months.* • *The monolingual Spanish-speaking seniors who access the services of our center for the first time within the grant period will increase by 50%.* • *A minimum of 50 Latino seniors in our new healthy Mexican food cooking class will learn how to cook healthier versions of the meals they love and eat most often.* • *Our referrals of Latino seniors from the community clinics and partnering nonprofit organizations specifically serving the Latino community will increase by 50% within the grant period.*

WORKSHEET 3.1B:
Statement of Need Questionnaire Example (Continued)

Who? Where? When?	What? Why?	Evidence of Problem	Impact If Problem Is Resolved?
When is the need evident?	Why does this need exist?		How is the need linked to your organization?
• *When these individuals have no "medical home," when they can't manage their chronic illnesses, and/or when they are socially isolated.*	• *No culturally competent organizations are serving this senior population. It has essentially been ignored.* • *Many in this segment of our member audience are living at or below the federal poverty line and therefore cannot purchase such services elsewhere.*		• *Our center's mission is to help seniors improve and maintain a healthy and independent lifestyle and to maximize their quality of life.*

Need Statement Review Questions

Once you have completed your need statement, answer the following six questions to see if what you've developed hits the mark:

1. Is your need statement focused on those you plan to serve (and not on your organization)?

2. Does your need statement directly connect to your organization's mission statement?

3. Given your organization's size and resources, can it meet the need in a meaningful way?

4. Is your need statement adequately supported by solid and reputable quantitative and qualitative data on the nature, size, and scope of the need to be addressed?

5. Have you practiced KISSing (Keeping It Sweet and Simple)?

6. Is your need statement persuasive without being wordy?

Your program's need is now established—you are on a roll. So keep it going by diving right into the goals and objectives section of your proposal.

Step 4

Defining Clear Goals and Objectives

Not all proposals get funded. Not all good proposals get funded. Not all good *programs* get funded (that is not redundant—those are three different concepts). Funders weigh priorities against a variety of factors when considering a proposal, including importance, significance, relevance and "so-what." The last item means, "So what if we fund this project and it succeeds—what will be better as a result?" Too often, grantseekers forget to explain these things simply through solid and well-articulated goals and objectives.

—EDWARD B. KACIC, MBA, CAIA
President & CEO
Irvine Health Foundation

IN THIS STEP you will learn the concept of writing clear goals and objectives. You will also focus on the important differences between them. Using a worksheet and following the examples, you will construct goals and a set of objectives for your own proposal.

Purpose of the Goals and Objectives Component: The "So What?" Factor

Once you have clearly defined the need your organization is trying to address, the next step is to develop solid goals that clearly define what the organization is trying to accomplish through its program and also to establish measurable objectives that will indicate the organization's progress toward its goals.

Content of the Goals and Objectives Component

Organization goals, including program and operating goals, are often written as part of a nonprofit's strategic planning process. Your organization's goals may already be developed and therefore ready for you to use. A funder will want to know the goals that relate directly to the stated need, so those goals should be included in this section of the proposal.

Definition

Goal. "A goal is a focus of accomplishment supported by a series of objectives needed to realize it or a broadly-stated subsidiary result."

For example, one goal of the Senior Latino Community Outreach Pilot Project is "to be the most inclusive, responsive, and culturally competent center for seniors in all of the communities who need our services."

Like goals, objectives are tied to the need statement.

Definition

Objectives. "An objective is a significant step toward a goal; or a precise, measurable, time-phased result." Objectives are much narrower than goals. There are two types of objectives. An outcome objective demonstrates an impact or result. A process objective focuses on a process to achieve the impact. Here are two examples from the Senior Latino Community Outreach Pilot Project:

Outcome objective example. "Ensure that a minimum of 75 Spanish-speaking seniors with Type II diabetes who complete our disease management classes maintain stabilized blood sugar levels for three consecutive months."

Process objective example. "The number of monolingual Spanish-speaking seniors who access the services of our center for the first time within the grant period will increase by 50%."

The exercises in this workbook focus specifically on outcome objectives.

As you prepare the objectives component of the proposal, keep the following in mind:

- Objectives should be stated in quantifiable terms.

- Outcome objectives should be stated in terms of outcomes, not activities or process. (Program activities and process are covered in Step Five, methods.)

- Objectives should specify the result of an activity.

- Objectives should clearly identify the target audience or community being served.

- Objectives should be realistic and capable of being accomplished within the time frame indicated, which is typically the grant period (most often one year in duration).

Do not fret; everyone struggles in the beginning with the differences between goals and objectives. Use this side-by-side comparison as an aid.

Goals Are	Objectives Are
Broad	Narrow
General intentions	Precise intentions
Intangible	Tangible
Abstract	Concrete
Cannot be validated as is	Can be validated

If you look at the writing of outcome objectives from an ends-and-means perspective, these objectives are the ends, whereas the methods (Step Five) are the means of reaching those ends. When developing each objective, answering the following five questions will help you clearly articulate the result your organization expects to accomplish:

1. What is (are) the key area(s) your organization is seeking to change?

2. What segment of the population will be involved in the change?

3. What is the direction of the change (an increase or improvement, or a decrease or reduction) your organization will be looking for?

4. What is the degree or amount of change your organization will be looking for?

5. What is the deadline for reaching that degree of change?

Definition

Methods, also known as strategies. "The methods that the organization will use to deliver services and implement activities in order to achieve its goals."

Remember the logic models briefly introduced back in Step One? Well, this step further illustrates the usefulness of incorporating a logic model in the program design. Applying the logic model in Resource C of this Workbook to the goals and objectives of the Senior Latino Community Outreach Pilot Project:

- The process objectives are in the *outputs* component.
- The outcome objectives are in the *outcomes* component.
- The goals are in the *impact* component.

Helpful Hint

Use the following phrases to assist you in framing your organization's program objectives appropriately:

To reduce   *To increase*   *To decrease*   *To expand*

Tips for Writing Good Goals and Objectives

- *Make sure goals and objectives tie directly to the need statement.* This is critical.

- *Include all relevant parties in the target population.*

- *Allow plenty of time for the objectives to be accomplished.* Things always take longer than planned.

- *Remember that outcome objectives do not describe methods.* Collaborating with the community clinics within the service area of the Some City Senior Center is a *method.* Stabilizing the blood sugar levels of a minimum of seventy-five monolingual Spanish-speaking seniors for three consecutive months is an *outcome objective,* as it describes the result of a method.

- *Determine how your organization is going to measure the change projected in each objective.* If you find you have no way to measure change, you probably need to rethink the objectives (more on this in Step Five). Measurement of the objective stated in the previous point might be described this way: "We will measure all participants' blood sugar levels at the beginning of the diabetes management classes and then measure their blood sugar levels weekly for three months following their completion of the classes to determine whether their blood sugar levels are stabilized."

- *Always try to write at least one outcome objective into your plan, and determine how you will measure it.* Remember to budget for evaluation activities if measuring the objective(s) will have costs associated with it.

Use Worksheet 4.1A to prepare to write your goals and objectives by focusing on outcomes. Start by writing down the goal of the program. Then describe the objectives that tie to that goal. Use the filled-out Worksheet 4.1B as a guide.

If your organization has more than one goal for its program, use a separate copy of Worksheet 4.1A for each goal. Limit the objectives to no more than four per goal.

Then write your proposal's goals and objectives component, following the standard formula supplied at the end of the worksheet, and using the sample goals and objectives on Worksheet 4.1B as a guide. When you are finished, go through the Goals and Objectives Review Questions, in the same way you did with the review questions for your statement of need. Remember, you want to be able to answer yes to each question in the review questions.

WORKSHEET 4.1A:
Goals and Objectives Exercise

Worksheet 4.1B contains sample goals and objectives. Please use it as an example as you complete this questionnaire.

GOAL:

	Objective 1	Objective 2	Objective 3	Objective 4
Direction of change				
Area of change				
Target population				
Degree of change				
Time frame				

Follow this standard form as you write out your objective statements: To (direction of change) + (area of change) + (target population) + (degree of change) + (time frame).

Winning Grants Step by Step, Third Edition. Copyright © 2008 by John Wiley & Sons, Inc. All rights reserved.

WORKSHEET 4.1B:
Goals and Objectives Exercise Example

GOAL: *Provide comprehensive access to health and social services for the seniors in the Latino communities served by our center.*

	Objective 1	Objective 2	Objective 3	Objective 4
Direction of change	*Increase*	*Increase*	*Increase*	*Increase*
Area of change	*Latino seniors with Type II diabetes*	*Monolingual Spanish-speaking seniors accessing our center*	*Latino seniors cooking healthy Mexican food*	*Referrals from partnering organizations*
Target population	*Spanish-speaking seniors with Type II diabetes*	*Monolingual Spanish-speaking seniors accessing our center for the first time*	*Latino seniors who still prepare their own meals*	*Our partnering organizations in the community who provide us with referrals*
Degree of change	*Minimum of 75 individuals*	*50%*	*Minimum of 50 individuals*	*50%*
Time frame	*6 months (3 months for classes and 3 months for maintenance)*	*12 months*	*12 months*	*12 months*

Follow this standard form as you write out your objective statements: To (direction of change) + (area of change) + (target population) + (degree of change) + (time frame).

Winning Grants Step by Step, Third Edition. Copyright © 2008 by John Wiley & Sons, Inc. All rights reserved.

Goals and Objectives Review Questions

1. Are your organization's goals stated as results?

2. Are your organization's outcome objectives stated as specific results that relate to a program goal?

3. Can progress in meeting your organization's objectives be quantified and assessed?

4. Do your organization's objectives describe the client population and a specific time frame for change?

Your nonprofit's need statement is in order, and you have the "so what?" factor covered in the program's goals and objectives. Let's move on to the development of your organization's methods, which is Step Five.

Step 5

Developing the Methods

It may not sound exciting, but a program which addresses a concrete community need, along with a solid implementation plan—goals, objectives and methods—is what we are looking for each and every time. Of course we are also looking for the inclusion of a realistic timeline as a part of that, which to us speaks directly to the ability of the organization to be successful.

—JULIE FARKAS
Senior Program Officer
Consumer Health Foundation

IN THIS STEP you will determine the methods your organization will use to reach its objectives. You will look at the elements of the methods component of a proposal and learn how to use a timeline so that you and your prospective funders can more easily see what will happen when. Using a worksheet and examples, you will write your methods for the objectives you developed in Step Four.

Purpose of the Methods Component

The need statement is clearly articulated, and the goals and objectives are set. The methods component of the proposal systematically walks grantmakers through the activities your organization proposes to carry out in order to accomplish its objectives.

Content of the Methods Component

Methods—also frequently referred to as activities or strategies—are detailed descriptions of the activities an organization will implement to achieve the ends specified in its objectives. Whatever you call them, this section of the proposal should clearly spell out the methods to be used and give the reasons for choosing them. Any research supporting the use of these methods—such as their previous success (either at your nonprofit or elsewhere) or, if the methods are untested, data that support your assertion that these methods might prove successful—should be included. This section should also address whether the methods selected are already in place within your organization and simply being "redeployed" to the program, or whether they are new. Finally, this section should describe who will staff the program and their qualifications, and identify the client population to be served, along with a justification of why this population was selected.

To develop the methods component, answer the following questions:

1. What are the elements that are inflexible (such as date of completion, dollars available, staffing needed)?

2. What activities need to be carried out in order to meet the objectives?

3. What are the starting and ending dates of these activities?

4. Who has responsibility for completing each activity?

5. How will participants be selected? (This question is not applicable to all projects.)

6. How was this methodology determined to be the best one to solve the problem presented? Does it build on models already in existence, or is it a different approach? If it is different, why is it different? And why did your organization select it?

The methods section should be realistic—the organization should be able to complete the proposed activities within the time frame stated in the proposal using the available resources. For proposals with multiple objectives and methods, it is a good idea to include a timeline showing when each method will start and finish. The accompanying Sample Timeline for the Some City Senior Center's Senior Latino Community Outreach Pilot Project shows one way to chart a nonprofit's activities on a timeline.

Going back to the logic model example in Resource C, the methods for the Senior Latino Community Outreach Pilot Project would be called activities in this model.

Tips for Writing the Methods Component

- Sync your organization's methods to the program's objectives and need statement.

- Tie your methods to the resources you are requesting in the program budget. Each activity should match its corresponding cost exactly.

- Explain the rationale for choosing these methods; talk in terms of research findings, expert opinion, and the organization's past experience with similar programs.

- Spell out the facilities and capital equipment that will be available for the project.

Sample Timeline (Abbreviated Version)

Activity	Month	1	2	3	4	5	6	7	8	9	10	11	12
1. Hire the project assistant.		X											
2. Recruit members of the outreach committee.			X										
3. Identify and retain the cultural competency consultant.				X									
4. Organize and host the first collaborative meeting with the center's partners.					X								
5. Hire the bilingual nurse.					X								
6. Develop and finalize the outreach strategies for client recruitment.						X							
7. Finalize the evaluation tools for the project.						X							
8. Officially launch the project with a public event that will feature prominent Latino community members in addition to center leadership.						X	X						
9. Evaluate and document progress toward objectives.				X			X			X			X

- Build various activity phases on top of one another to move the effort toward the desired results. Include a timeline.

- Be sure to discuss who will be served and how they will be chosen.

- Do not assume the program officer knows more than any woman on the street is likely to know about your nonprofit or what you propose.

Look over the Sample Methods Component for the Some City Senior Center's project. Then develop your organization's methods by completing Worksheet 5.1A, which asks you to list the key elements of the organization's planned program. Consult Worksheet 5.1B, which contains an example of a completed list of methods, as necessary. Then use the Sample Methods Component as a guide as you write your own methods section for your proposal. (The sample shows the methods for one objective. Additional objectives would be handled the same way.) Finally, use the Methods Review Questions to review your organization's methods, just as you did for your organization's need statement and goals and objectives.

Sample Methods Component

In order to achieve the objectives for our Senior Latino Community Outreach Pilot Project, Some City Senior Center will employ the methods outlined below. We have confidence in these methods, as they have been tested and proven successful by two of our fellow nonprofit organizations whose client populations are Latino: Health Access Latinos in Some City and the XYZ Community Clinic in Valley Vista. Representatives of both organizations served as advisers to us as we developed this pilot project. We have also prepared a detailed timeline, which is included in the appendixes to this proposal.

Objective One
Ensure that a minimum of 75 Spanish-speaking seniors with Type II diabetes who complete our disease management classes maintain stabilized blood sugar levels for three consecutive months.

Methods
- Some City Senior Center will hire a program assistant and a full-time bilingual nurse who specializes in chronic disease management. Establish an outreach committee cochaired by two of our Latino and/or Spanish-speaking board members and including diverse community representation (geography, race, ethnicity, gender, and occupation).

- The bilingual nurse and program assistant will adapt the center's current diabetes self-management classes, including classroom tools and materials, to make them linguistically and culturally appropriate for Spanish-speaking seniors.

- The bilingual nurse and program assistant will develop the protocols for testing and tracking program participants for three consecutive months after completing the classes.

- Staff will develop a formal referral system and feedback mechanism between our center and all appropriate community agencies positioned to provide referrals to our Spanish-speaking diabetes management classes.

- Staff will hold weekly Spanish language diabetes self-management classes.

- Staff will track participants' progress on a weekly basis for three months following completion of the classes.

- The program assistant will formally chart the progress of each participant.

WORKSHEET 5.1A:
Methods Exercise

Worksheet 5.1B illustrates how a completed methods exercise might look. Please use it as an example as you perform this exercise.

Task and Subtasks	Person(s) Responsible	Resources Needed	Start and Finish Dates

WORSHEET 5.1B: Methods Exercise Example			

Task and Subtasks	Person(s) Responsible	Resources Needed	Start and Finish Dates
Hire a program assistant and a full-time bilingual nurse.	Executive director	Funds for salaries and benefits; recruitment and hiring process; job descriptions	Within two months of project start-up for the PA; within four months of start-up for the nurse
Establish an outreach committee.	Executive director and program assistant	List of potential prospects; meeting space	Within one month of project start-up
Adapt the center's current diabetes self-management classes to ensure they are linguistically and culturally appropriate.	Bilingual nurse and program assistant	Language consultant specializing in translation; updated materials from current classes; funds for consultant	Within three months of start-up
Develop the protocols for testing and tracking program participants for three consecutive months after completing the classes.	Bilingual nurse and program assistant	Information on best practices for data tracking and collection; computer and software	Within four months of start-up
Develop a formal referral system and feedback mechanism.	Executive director, outreach committee cochairs, and program assistant	Information on best practices for referral systems and feedback mechanisms	Within five months of start-up
Organize weekly Spanish language diabetes self-management classes.	Bilingual nurse and program assistant	Meeting space; self-management educational materials; refreshments	Within six months of start-up
Track participants' progress on a weekly basis for three months following completion of the classes.	Bilingual nurse and program assistant	Filing cabinet; file folders and office supplies; computer; private office for weekly screenings	Starting week nine of grant period

Methods Review Questions

1. Do the methods discussed in the proposal derive logically from the need statement and the goals and objectives?

2. Do the methods present the program activities to be undertaken?

3. Have you explained why you selected the specific methods or activities?

4. Have you explained the timing and order of the specific activities?

5. Is it clear who will perform specific activities?

6. Given the organization's projected resources, are the proposed activities feasible?

If you have been following along with each step, including testing each of your proposal components against the questions at the end of each, you are now in prime position to be successful in the next step: developing your evaluation component.

Step 6

Preparing the Evaluation Component

EVERYTHING YOU HAVE completed in the development of your organization's proposal (needs assessment, goals, objectives, and methods) naturally leads you to this component, as evaluation answers questions that both your organization and the funder have, such as

- Was the program successful?

- Did we do what we set out to do?

- What impact did the program have on the community or target audience?

- What did we learn from this experience that can be leveraged?

- What didn't work—and why or why not?

- What's different as a result of our program?

As you prepare the goals, objectives, and methods, it is now more important than ever to plan how your organization will evaluate what it proposes to do. In this step you will learn how to write an evaluation plan so that your organization can effectively demonstrate the success of its program and measure program impact—and also capture the lessons learned. An exercise will help you think about what your evaluation plan should contain.

Definitions

Impact. "The fundamental intended or unintended long-term change occurring in organizations, communities, or systems as a result of program activities."

Leverage. "A method of grantmaking practiced by some foundations. Leverage occurs when a small amount of money is given with the express purpose of attracting funding from other sources or of providing the organization with the tools it needs to raise other kinds of funds." Leverage may also be defined as building momentum from one effort to the next.

Purpose of the Evaluation Component

Evaluation is a process that determines the impact, effectiveness, and efficiency of a program. It reveals what worked and—equally important—what did not. Decisions made during this process can help the organization plan for the program's future, and the process can produce an organized and objective report documenting the *return on investment* for funders and the realized benefits to the community the organization serves. How a program will be evaluated must be determined prior to implementation so that the organization can build evaluation measurements into the final program plan. Always keep in mind that funders expect to hear from organizations how they define and measure the success of a program.

Definition

Return on Investment (ROI). "The amount of benefit (return) based on the amount of resources (funds) used to produce it."

Specific Virtues of Evaluation

First, a good evaluation component strengthens the proposal from the program officer's perspective. You are asking potential grantmakers to invest in your project—and you are asking the program officer to be your advocate. You want the funding institution to bet on the fact that the world as your nonprofit sees it will be improved in some specific way as a result of the proposed program. Essentially, proposed programs serve to test a hypothesis—"If we do this, then that will happen." A solid evaluation component in a proposal reassures a funder that the organization is interested, as the funder is, in learning whether this hypothesis is correct.

Second, through evaluation, your organization will learn about the program's strengths and areas of weakness. The process alone of thinking through the evaluation design can strengthen a program before it's even implemented. From there your organization can take the knowledge gained through an actual evaluation and share it with staff and volunteers to improve programs as they are being implemented—a strategy often referred

---

Definition

Hypothesis. "The assumed proposition that is tested in a research process."

---

to as a midcourse correction. This knowledge may also be shared with others in the field so that they, too, can learn the lessons of the program's work.

The third benefit is to the public—the impact. Dollars granted from foundations and corporate giving programs are dollars dedicated to charitable good; therefore, with each grant you become a recipient of public trust once again. Because of that, your organization has an obligation to ensure that its programs are actually having a positive impact on the community as a whole or on the target audience that it purports to serve within the community. Evaluation is one of the strongest and most effective tools any nonprofit has to verify and document that it is indeed fulfilling its obligation to make a positive impact on the community it serves.

Internal or External Evaluation

Most foundations typically allow organizations to designate from 5 to 10 percent of the total program budget for evaluation. You need to consider what the most effective use of those funds would be. Some organizations will spend time up front, crystallizing their evaluation components and coming to feel confident that they have both the staffing and the expertise in place to objectively and thoroughly handle the evaluation internally. Other organizations will decide to engage an outside evaluator, for any number of reasons (lacking expertise among the staff and wanting the evaluation to be deemed as objective as it can be are two of the most common). In either case you should provide some background information in your proposal indicating which direction you intend to take.

Content of the Evaluation Component

The ability to fully understand both the big picture of your program and the individual pieces that make up that big picture is a must. Evaluation design requires dedicated thinking. First, you need to consider your organization's definition of success—the "so what?" factor. Then you must determine the relationship between the expected outcomes and the activities described in the proposal. Finally, you need to identify the most important aspects of the program, then identify why it is important to evaluate them.

Organizations conduct evaluations primarily to accomplish six purposes:

1. Find out whether or not the hypothesis was correct: Did what the organization originally proposed actually do what the organization expected that it would?

2. Determine if the methods that were specified were indeed used and the objectives met.

3. Determine if an impact was made on the need identified.

4. Obtain feedback from the clients served and other members of the community.

5. Maintain some control over the project.

6. Make midcourse corrections along the way to increase the program's chances of success.

When preparing the evaluation section of the proposal, answering the following questions will help you frame what you will say:

1. What is the purpose of your organization's evaluation?

2. How will the findings be used?

3. What will you know after the evaluation that you do not know now?

4. What will you do after the evaluation that you cannot do now because of lack of information?

5. How will the lives of the people or community you serve be better?

The focus of this workbook, as in previous editions, does not allow for detailed information on program evaluation methods. A free resource you should consider reviewing as an accompaniment to this workbook is the *W. K. Kellogg Foundation Evaluation Handbook*, which can be found on the foundation's website (www.wkkf.org).

That said, here is a broad overview that can provide some assistance as you determine the parameters most appropriate for your project. Generally, there are two approaches to data collection: quantitative methods and qualitative methods.

Quantitative methods are, as their name implies, methods to quantify (measure or count) data. They directly answer the question, "How much did we do?" Using this method, you collect data that you can analyze statistically, using averages, means, percentiles, and the like. These analyses allow you to make statements about cause-and-effect relationships. Employ quantitative methods for questions focused on

- Understanding the quantities or frequency of particular aspects of a program (such as number of enrollees or number of dropouts)

- Determining whether a cause-and-effect relationship is present

- Comparing two different methods seeking to achieve the same outcomes
- Establishing numerical baselines (through such means as pretests, posttests, and quarterly or yearly follow-ups)

Qualitative methods, in contrast, are based on direct contact with the people involved with a program. These methods consist of interviews (group or individual), observation (direct or field), and review of selected documents. According to the Nonprofit Good Practice Guide Glossary (www.npgoodpractice.org/Glossary), this approach "implies an emphasis on processes and meanings that are rigorously examined, but not measured in terms of quantity, amount, or frequency." Employ qualitative methods for questions focused on

- Understanding feelings or opinions about a program among participants, staff, or community members
- Gaining insight into how patterns of relationships in the program unfold
- Gathering multiple perspectives to understand the whole picture
- Identifying approximate indicators that clients are moving in the "right" direction

In other words, pretests and posttests are not the only measures of success. By taking the time to think clearly and strategically up front, an organization can come up with a creative and valuable evaluation design that incorporates both quantitative and qualitative methods. For example, Some City Senior Center staff might use a pretest and posttest (quantitative method) to measure each new Spanish-speaking member's individual success in grasping the new diabetes management protocols being taught in the new diabetes management classes, and they might also observe the classroom and the facility in which the curriculum is taught to better understand each member's experience (qualitative method).

The evaluation component should highlight the data collection methods you plan to employ for the program. Like every other component of the proposal, the evaluation should connect directly with both the objectives and the methods. If your objectives and methods were crafted as recommended—meaning they are measurable and time-specific—that will make the task of preparing a good data collection plan and proposal evaluation much easier.

Take a look at the Sample Evaluation Component prepared for the Senior Latino Community Outreach Pilot Project.

Sample Evaluation Component

Our formal referral system and feedback mechanism will serve a dual purpose. First, we can track all referrals of new Latino seniors, which services we are able to provide, and where the referrals are coming from. Second, our feedback loop will allow us to gather information about member satisfaction with our services, which we will review every other month. This is of particular importance since one of our objectives with the program is to grow and institutionalize our collective cultural competence. The satisfaction reports will allow us to fine-tune our outreach and newly developed Spanish language program offerings.

Specific to our diabetes self-management class, we will employ a combination of evaluation tools. We will use pretests and posttests with every new monolingual Spanish-speaking senior who participates in the classes. We will also take the blood sugar level of each new senior at the beginning of the classes, and monitor each senior's blood sugar level once weekly for three months upon completion of the classes. This monitoring will be done by the nurse, who will use a glucometer to measure each participant's levels. The medical readings will be documented in the client's file every week for three months to determine whether participation in the self-management classes has an effect on the seniors' ability to successfully manage their blood sugar levels and therefore effectively manage their diabetes.

Answer the questions in Worksheet 6.1A to begin planning your evaluation section. The sample answers in Worksheet 6.1B will help you get started. Be sure to refer to the Sample Evaluation Component before writing the organization's evaluation section. When you complete your evaluation section, review it with the Evaluation Review Questions.

WORKSHEET 6.1A:
Evaluation Planning Questionnaire

Worksheet 6.1B contains sample answers to these questions. Please use it as an example as you complete this questionnaire.

1. What questions will your organization's evaluation activities seek to answer?

2. What are the specific evaluation plans and time frames?

    a. What kinds of data will be collected?

    b. At what points?

    c. Using what strategies or instruments?

    d. Using what comparison group or baseline, if any?

3. If you intend to study a sample of participants, how will this sample be constructed?

4. What procedures will you use to determine whether the program was implemented as planned?

5. Who will conduct the evaluation?

6. Who will receive the results?

7. How are you defining success for this program or project?

WORKSHEET 6.1B:
Evaluation Planning Questionnaire Example

1. What questions will the program's evaluation activities seek to answer?

    Are the objectives of the program being met?

    Is the Latino community responding to our outreach?

    Are we becoming more culturally competent as an organization?

2. What are the specific evaluation plans and time frames?

    a. What kinds of data will be collected?

    Numbers of Latino seniors in our service area coming to our center for the first time

    Numbers of monolingual Spanish-speaking seniors accessing our new language and culture-appropriate programming

    Satisfaction levels of those participating in our new programming

    Key health indicators

    b. At what points?

    Weekly for some; monthly for others

    c. Using what strategies or instruments?

    Pretests and posttests

    Database tracking systems

    Our formal feedback mechanism

    Medical records

    Interviews and focus groups

    d. Using what comparison group or baseline, if any?

    Last year's numbers of clients served

    Medical records

WORKSHEET 6.1B:
Evaluation Planning Questionnaire Example (Continued)

3. If you intend to study a sample of participants, how will this sample be constructed?

   N/A

4. What procedures will you use to determine whether the program was implemented as planned?

   Monthly review of our detailed program implementation timeline, which incorporates all our specified methods

5. Who will conduct the evaluation?

   The program assistant, with support from the cultural competency consultant

6. Who will receive the reports?

   All staff

   Referring partners

   Our board

   Our funding partners

7. How are you defining success for this program or project?

   Meeting our objectives as outlined in the proposal will be our initial definition of success. Beyond the first year, the center will define success as continuing referrals from our partnering organizations; positive feedback from our Latino members via our formal feedback mechanism; and incorporation of this project into our operating budget.

Evaluation Review Questions

1. Does the evaluation section focus on assessing the project results?

2. Does it describe how the evaluation will assess the efficiency of program methods?

3. Does it describe who will be evaluated and what will be measured?

4. Does it state what information will be collected in the evaluation process?

5. Does it state who will be responsible for making the assessments?

6. Does it discuss how the information and conclusions will be used to improve the program?

7. Does it provide the organization's definition of success?

If the program is successful and you are able to document that success through evaluation, you are probably going to want that program to continue. Step Seven addresses the need to plan now for program sustainability beyond the initial funding.

Developing Sustainability Strategies

IN THIS STEP you will learn how to develop strategies to continue the program beyond the initial grant funding. Other resources are available to keep programs running, but your organization must position itself early to take full advantage of—to leverage—the first grant(s). You will identify, through exercises and examples, the potential sources of ongoing support that are best for the project.

Purpose of the Sustainability Component

The purpose of this component is to help you consider how the program will be funded past its immediate future. Potential funders want to know that you are thinking beyond their funding; they want to know your plans for the time when their funding comes to an end—and it will. How will your organization continue the good work upon which the community has come to depend? The old saying "last but not least" applies well here: this might be the last section of narrative in the proposal, but it is by no means the least important.

Content of the Sustainability Component

The sustainability component needs to reflect whether the proposal is seeking program, capital or equipment, or capacity-building funding. Then it must address how the program will continue once the grant comes to a close. When a program ends prematurely, it typically leaves "unfinished business." In other words, it fails to achieve its intended goals and therefore does not successfully address the need outlined at the beginning of the proposal. *And let's not forget the ultimate impact this has on the clients, constituents, and community who are counting on this program.* For that reason, funders pay much more attention to this section than most nonprofits would probably suspect because—like you—they will have a vested interest in the project's success. So this section of your proposal should provide a framework that shows how your nonprofit plans to continue the program beyond the funder's initial investment, as well as who on your staff will be responsible for making this plan happen.

In capital or equipment proposals (major equipment purchases or building renovations and expansion) grantmakers need to know what the associated costs are for operating the new equipment, for maintaining the new building, or for increasing services if building expansion results in program expansion. They need this information because these are all costs that the organization will incur beyond the funding being requested. You will also need to show that the sources of funding meet these additional costs.

In the case of a capacity-building grant, funders want to know how the nonprofit will support the capacity it has grown. For example, you might have requested a capacity-building grant to increase the organization's fundraising ability via the creation of a development plan. Once the plan is created—and the grant is expended—how do you plan to pay for the actual implementation of your new development plan?

Consider future funding from one or more of these sources:

- *Continuation grants from foundations and corporations.* A nonprofit can seek continuing support from those foundations and corporations that fund ongoing programs. However, as we stated earlier, a majority of foundation and corporate funders prefer to support new and expanding programs—not continuation funding for existing programs.

- *Annual campaigns.* Organizations can develop fundraising campaigns whose revenues are restricted to a program's operational costs.

- *Fees for service.* If a nonprofit opts to ask clients to pay fees, the fee scale and a revenue plan should be shown in the proposal.

- *Sales of items or activities.* A nonprofit might be able to set up an income-producing program, such as a gift shop or thrift store. In addition, it might be able to sell publications, concert recordings, or educational activities. Revenues generated from these sales might cover some costs of the program. If this route is taken, a clear expense and revenue projection should be a part of the proposal. (Please note: *You need to check with both legal counsel and accounting counsel to ensure that any revenue-generating ventures you launch are set up and monitored in accordance with IRS standards.*)

A typical mistake that grantseekers make in their proposals is not taking this component as seriously as they should and not fully understanding that grant funding does in fact come to an end. Saying something to the

---

Helpful Hint

Toot your own horn! If you have examples to share of other instances in which the organization successfully continued programs beyond their initial funding, this would be the place to share such information, because it speaks to your organization's credibility not only in launching programs but also in maintaining them, which in the end is truly the hardest part of the work.

---

effect of "future funding will come from a mix of sources such as other grants and individual support" is not a sustainability plan that plays well to grantmakers.

Tips for Writing the Sustainability Component

Many funders ask specifically for this component in their grant guidelines; others do not. Whether or not this component is required, you should include some information on sources of support for the project's future.

The more specific you are in this section, the more confidence you will inspire in potential funders that the project will continue beyond their grant, maximizing the impact of their investment.

Take a look at the Sample Sustainability Component to see what the Some City Senior Center has planned for the sustainability of its program.

Answering the questions in Worksheet 7.1A will get you started on developing the future funding component of your proposal. Worksheet 7.1B provides sample answers, continuing the example of the Senior Latino Community Outreach Pilot Project. Then write your own future funding information, referring to the Sample Sustainability Component you reviewed earlier. Check your work by answering the Sustainability Review Questions.

Sample Sustainability Component

The Some City Senior Center has a successful fourteen-year track record of securing and maintaining funding for its numerous programs and services. We anticipate receiving a portion of the program's funding from the city governments of Some City, Valley Vista, Grove Beach, and Hill Viejo, as well as from the Any County government. We also have two board members—the same board members who have stepped forward to cochair our program's outreach committee—who have committed $2,500 each for three years. Our board and staff believe so strongly in this program that they have committed to helping our director of development to raise an additional $25,000 per year in our annual fundraising campaigns specifically for this program. Finally, we are in continuing conversations with the Wegivit Foundation and Youtakeit Regional Fund, as both have provided small grants to assist us in piloting the project. These two local grantmakers have indicated clearly that they have an interest in potentially larger investments should we move forward with the program after our pilot year.

WORKSHEET 7.1A:
Future Funding Questionnaire

Worksheet 7.1B contains sample answers to these questions. Please use it as an example as you complete this questionnaire.

Risks and Opportunities	Sources of Future Financial Resources	Internal Requirements
Do we intend to continue this project?	What sources can we use?	What internal plans do we have for obtaining future funding?
For how long?		
What resources (direct and indirect) are needed?		

WORKSHEET 7.1B:
Future Funding Questionnaire Example

Risks and Opportunities	Sources of Future Financial Resources	Internal Requirements
Do we intend to continue this project? • *Yes*	What sources can we use? • *Our own budget via annual fundraising* • *City government (four cities)* • *County government* • *In-kind corporate contributions*	What internal plans do we have for obtaining future funding? • *Incorporating a portion of the program's expenses into our center's operating budget* • *Continuing our collaboration with partnering nonprofit agencies to provide referrals* • *Submitting collaborative proposals for funding with our partnering agencies* • *Raising additional funding that would be restricted to this program through our agency development efforts* • *Securing in-kind corporate contributions from businesses that either already specifically cater to the Latino community or want to broaden their reach to the Latino community*
For how long? • *As long as it is needed*		
What resources (direct and indirect) are needed? • *Culturally competent staff and bilingual staff* • *Committed board* • *Equipment* • *Meeting and working space* • *Clients* • *Funding partners*		

Sustainability Review Questions

1. Is it your organization's intent to have the program continue after the initial grant funding is gone?

2. If yes, does the sustainability component of your proposal present a plan for securing future funding for the program?

3. Does it discuss future funding strategies or earned-income strategies?

4. If you are requesting a multiyear grant, have you shown that your organization will have a decreasing reliance on grant support each year? (Grantmakers are more inclined to make a multiyear grant to nonprofits that assume greater financial responsibility for the project each year, rather than asking the funder to maintain the same level of funding each year.)

Now it's time to translate your nonprofit's program into the language of dollars by developing a budget.

Step 8

Preparing the Program Budget

I am most pleased when I read about a great program followed by a strong proposal that directly supports the program. The proposal is ultimately bolstered by a well-articulated budget. Many times my colleagues and I will read the executive summary of a proposal first, followed by a review of the budget to see if they are accurately reflective of each other—before we dive into the full proposal. We need to see that your budget is reasonable, logical, and is well-connected to what you are proposing. Be mindful of your overhead—and be knowledgeable about what your overhead costs are, just in case you are asked.

—PHYLLIS CALDWELL

President

Washington Area Women's Foundation

(a public grantmaking charity in Washington, D.C.)

THIS STEP HELPS you estimate how much your program will cost and introduces you to the key elements of a program budget. Examples aid you in defining budget elements and guidelines for budget preparation are provided.

Purpose of the Program Budget

Put simply, a program budget is the program plan from a financial point of view. This definition is borrowed from *Grant Seeker's Budget Toolkit,* by James Aaron Quick and Cheryl Carter New, a solid and in-depth resource for anyone who needs more specific knowledge or guidance about preparing budgets. The best budgets directly translate the methods section of the proposal into dollars—words into numbers. For example, a budget typically includes the number and cost of staff and volunteers needed to implement the program plan, as described in the proposal. Always remember that the program budget is your best "guesstimate"—a projection—of the income and expenses you anticipate for your program.

Definition

Projection. "A prediction or estimate of future conditions, based on present data or trends."

Content of the Budget

In most instances you will be asked to submit your organization's operating budget for the current fiscal year, so be prepared by having copies handy. You will also need to submit a budget specific to the funding request you are making. For a program support grant, you will be asked to develop a budget outlining all expenses and revenues associated with that specific program. If a nonprofit is seeking operating or general support, you should submit the budget for the whole agency along with a request for unrestricted funds. This will serve as your "program" budget. Depending on the funding source, you may be asked either for a very detailed budget or for a general outline of income and expenses.

Definition

Unrestricted funds. Funds "not specifically designated for a particular use by the donor, or for which restrictions have expired or been removed." Also known as operating or general support funds.

Whereas government funding sources often require considerable financial detail and provide instructions and budget forms that you must use, many foundations and corporations require less detail than this. They still, however, give serious consideration to your budget as they evaluate the merit of the proposal. In a trend currently growing in popularity, more and more grantmakers are now including a budget template among their guidelines. (Some samples of this approach are included on the CD accompanying this workbook.) Even when a funder says the budget template is optional, you should use it. It is also always time well spent to call the foundation to which you are applying to speak with someone about the budget, if at all possible, because he may provide additional information and clarity about funder expectations. For example, you might learn that although a funder excludes equipment *purchases* from consideration, it does permit equipment *leasing*.

A budget may be one or more of these types:

- *Program (or project) budget:* the income and expenses associated with the specific program for which the nonprofit is seeking funding.

- *Agency budget:* the income and expenses projected for your whole organization, inclusive of all its programs.

- *Detailed or justified budget:* a high level of detail about certain income and expenses items; also sometimes referred to as a budget narrative or justification.

- *In-kind contribution budget:* the donated goods and services expected to be used in a specific program or elsewhere in the organization. This budget is commonly prepared as part of a program, agency, or detailed budget.

The level of detail you need to supply in your budget will vary from funder to funder and from program to program. In rare instances a grant-maker may not require a budget if the funds are to be used for a specific item—such as to purchase a single piece of equipment or food or tickets for a particular event.

Tips for Developing the Budget

To develop the budget component of a proposal for a program, follow these steps:

1. Establish the budget period, the length of time the budget covers.

2. Estimate expenses, obtaining cost estimates as necessary.

3. Decide whether and how to include overhead costs.

4. Estimate the donated goods and services that will be used.

5. Estimate the anticipated revenues for the project.

6. Check that the budget as a whole makes sense and conveys the right message to the funder, which is this: the budget is appropriate and in line with the objectives and methods of the program to be funded.

Establish the Budget Period

Are you proposing an eighteen-month program or a six-month project? You need to state clearly in your proposal what the grant period will be. Your budget will directly reflect that designated period by showing income and expenses for exactly that time.

If program implementation depends on obtaining funding, you will likely not know exactly when the program will start. Should this be the case, prepare a budget for the time period only, rather than for specific months—that is, if you are proposing a one-year grant, draw up your budget for one year without specifically identifying the starting or concluding months. Be mindful that the period for the program does not need to match your organization's fiscal year. However, if you are also submitting an agencywide budget, that document should be the actual budget for the current or upcoming fiscal year.

Estimate Expenses and Costs

Begin by estimating direct costs, expenses that are directly related—and indispensable—to the program. Such expenses typically include

- Program staff salaries and benefits
- Office space (which may be an assigned percentage, based on your program budget as a proportion of your organization's overall budget)
- Supplies (office, educational, and so forth)
- Equipment
- Program-related travel
- Program-related rent (percentage of nonprofit office space used)
- Printing and copying

Use the worksheet you filled out in Step Five (where you developed methods and a timeline) as the basis for calculating your program's direct expenses. For larger expenses, such as equipment or space rental, get some cost estimates so that you won't under- or overbudget on these large items. At this stage don't try to determine each item down to the last penny; make your best guess of how much it will cost to hire a good intake worker (remember to include the costs of benefits) or to design and print a program brochure. Use industry standards as your guide and you should be within the appropriate range. Not sure what industry standards are for some items? Ask a colleague, either one within your organization who runs another program or one at another nonprofit.

Calculate Overhead Costs

Indirect costs, often called overhead or administrative costs, are costs shared by all the organization's activities and programs, such as the cost of the audit, the executive director's salary, general liability insurance, the copier lease, and the phone system. Indirect costs are the nuts-and-bolts expenses that it takes to operate a nonprofit, yet are not specific to any one program (telephones, a postage meter, Internet access, electricity, and office machines are a few more examples).

Every program and special project at an organization benefits from agency functions that are classified as overhead costs. Therefore, including a portion of these costs in the request for funding has become fairly standard. A good place to begin, as always, is by reviewing the funder's guidelines. There is a good chance that the funder has specifically addressed its policy on overhead in this material; some funders will name the maximum percentage they will consider for overhead costs.

Although it is usually reasonable to include overhead costs, avoid the temptation to assign more overhead costs to a grant than are justified. Most foundations, when providing support for a specific program, do not want to pay for more than the program's fair share of these costs. Your research on the funder and conversations with the program officer should ultimately tell you what you can include.

Estimate Donated (In-Kind) Goods and Services

Never underestimate the benefits of donated goods and volunteer time, as they are important to many nonprofit ventures. If, for example, you receive in-kind copying from a board member and have a volunteer receptionist, the dollar costs of the program will be reduced.

Reality Check

Do not spread yourself too thin in this area. Be sure to verify your volunteer commitments as best you can—perhaps consider getting them (unofficially) in writing (via a memorandum of understanding) and submitting them as backup to the budget—in addition to building in a small contingency plan in case your in-kind support falls through.

Including in-kind contributions in your budget is helpful for several reasons:

- It allows the full scope and costs of the project to be understood by the funder.

- It demonstrates community support for your project and agency, which is very important to donors.

- It reminds you and the donors and volunteers of the value of their contributions.

Think about it this way: Why would a funder want to support your organization's program if you cannot demonstrate that your own community supports it?

In-kind contributions are usually shown as both income and expense, at the same levels. If, for example, your program receives $5,000 in in-kind printing and copying from a local business, your budget should also show an "expenditure," or cost, of $5,000 in printing and copying. If a volunteer teacher contributes $5,000 worth of her time, your organization should also record a payout of $5,000 in teaching expenses.

Estimate Anticipated Revenues

The power of leveraging should also not be underestimated. If you are applying to more than one funder for program support (as you absolutely should be doing!), you want to have that information reflected in your budget. Many times, funders feel more comfortable investing in programs along with their fellow funding institutions.

In addition, some programs will generate income through fees that can help pay program expenses. Other income may include individual contributions, a special event, or as just mentioned, grants from more than one source. Each possible source of revenue for the program should be estimated for the grant period and included in the budget.

As a general rule, funders expect to see a balanced budget for a project, one in which income and expenses are equal. Most grantmakers will likely shy away from supporting programs that are projected to end the grant period with either a large deficit or a major surplus of cash.

Helpful Hint

If your organization is sending requests to several foundations at once, it's to your benefit to let all of the funders know. Funders do talk to each other, so it is quite possible that you could leverage your chances of receiving grants if they all know up front whom you have approached. You might use language such as this: "In addition to your foundation, we are submitting this proposal to the ABC Foundation and the XYZ Foundation," or, "We have already received a grant of $25,000 from MNO Foundation, and are seeking to leverage this funding with a grant of $25,000 from your foundation. Together, these two grants would fully fund our program for the year."

Check for Sense

After preparing the initial budget, take a close look to ensure that it makes sense and corresponds closely to the methods you developed for your program back in Step Five. Make adjustments in income and expenses as appropriate, always keeping in mind that you do not want to raise any red flags. Take a step back and review the budget from an objective perspective: Is there anything that stands out? What is not clearly tied to the methods proposed? What raises your own eyebrows?

Use Worksheet 8.1A to prepare a budget for your project. Enter your projected revenues and expenses, and add categories if necessary and appropriate. Worksheet 8.1B contains a completed budget, which shows you what the budget for the Senior Latino Community Outreach Pilot Project looks like. Asking the Budget Review Questions at the end of this step will highlight those areas in your budget that need further attention.

WORKSHEET 8.1A:
Revenue and Expense Budget

Worksheet 8.1B contains a sample budget. Please use it as an example as you complete this budget worksheet.

	Cash Required	In-Kind Contributions	Total Budget
REVENUE			
Foundations			
Government			
Corporations			
Individual contributions			
Donated printing & supplies			
Volunteer services			
Other (specify):			
Total revenue			
EXPENSES			
Salaries (prorated if less than full-time)			
_____			
_____			
_____			
_____			
_____			
Payroll taxes & benefits (% of salaries)			
Bookkeeping contractor			
Other (specify):			
Total personnel			
Office rent (% for program)			
Supplies			
Printing			
Utilities			
Telephone			
Copy services			
Postage			
Travel			
Membership dues			
Other (specify):			
Total nonpersonnel			
Total expenses			

WORKSHEET 8.1B:
Revenue and Expense Budget Example

	Cash Required	In-Kind Contributions	Total Budget
REVENUE			
Foundations	$100,000		$100,000
Government	50,000		50,000
Corporations	25,000		25,000
Individual contributions	5,000		5,000
Donated printing & supplies		$5,000	5,000
Volunteer services		5,000	5,000
Other (specify):			
Total revenue	**$180,000**	**$10,000**	**$190,000**
EXPENSES			
Salaries (prorated if less than full-time)			
Bilingual nurse	50,000		
Program assistant	40,000		
Executive director (15%)	11,250		
Payroll taxes & benefits (32% of salaries)	32,400		
Cultural comp. consultant	12,400		
Other (specify):			
Total personnel	143,650		143,650
Volunteer services		5,000	
Supplies	2,500		
Printing		5,000	
Food & beverages for meetings	5,000		
Equipment (medical & computer)[a]	8,850		
Copy services	2,500		
Postage	1,300		
Conferences, travel, & mileage[b]	4,800		
Membership dues			
Overhead[c] at 10%	9,000		
Total nonpersonnel	$33,950	$10,000	$43,950
Total expenses	**$180,000**	**$10,000**	**$190,000**

[a] Includes computers for new staff, tracking software, medical supplies not donated in-kind.

[b] Includes sending three to the National Organization of La Raza conference in San Diego; all mileage costs associated with the project.

[c] Includes rent and all utilities, including telephone.

Budget Review Questions

1. Is the budget consistent with the proposal's program plan (methods)?

2. Is there a budget narrative that explains items that may not be immediately clear?

3. Does the budget include in-kind revenues and expenses?

4. Does the budget address the question of how overhead costs will be recovered?

5. Is the budget realistic? In other words, can your organization accomplish the intended objectives with the proposed budget?

6. Have you kept your budget worksheet, so that you have a record of how you determined costs for the expense items?

Writing the Organization Background Component

IN ADDITION TO the planning sections of the proposal, you need to develop a section about the organization itself. This step provides an overview of the purpose of an organization background section and of what it should contain to best establish your nonprofit's credibility. Using examples and a worksheet, you will learn how to present your organization's strengths to funders.

Purpose of the Organization Background Statement

What are the mission, values, and other distinguishing characteristics of your organization? And why will it be able to do what it is proposing successfully? The organization background component answers these questions and more. This is the section of the proposal where you get to tell funders all about your organization (and brag a little!), which means it can get rather lengthy if you don't use some restraint. *Try to limit this proposal component to no more than three pages.* A good organization background statement describes the nonprofit well enough to assure prospective funders that this nonprofit can successfully undertake the proposed program.

Grantmakers may refer to this section as the "Introduction" or the "Applicant Description," but the same basic information is expected regardless of its name. This section of your proposal should allow the reviewer to get a strong impression that your organization

- Is fiscally secure
- Is well managed
- Provides important community services
- Understands the community it serves
- Reflects that community in its board and staff
- Has the respect of the community

Content of the Organization Background Component

Starting with the basics, you will want to include the following:

- A description of the organization and its mission and vision, and how it came to be—its history.

- The demographics of the community your organization serves, followed by the ways in which both the board members and the staff reflect those demographics. This information is growing steadily in importance to funders, as they want to make sure that the nonprofit is in the best position to truly understand and connect with the community it says it serves.

- A description of the organization's position and role in the community. Who are the organization's collaborating partners in the community?

- A discussion of the ways the organization is unique in comparison to others providing similar services.

- Descriptions of innovative programs or special services the organization has provided. Has it received any awards or special recognition?

- A very *brief* history of funding by other sources.

Your primary goal in crafting this section of the proposal is to establish credibility with potential funders. You need to use your judgment as to what is appropriate given the specific proposal—and the funder. The guiding question should be, "What is the key information this funder needs about my organization and its qualifications to solidify the case for undertaking the proposed program?" For example, when seeking funds for a project that proposes to target outreach to recruit and work with monolingual Spanish-speaking seniors, it would be most beneficial to support the case by discussing the organization's history and experience of working with seniors and also its experience with innovative approaches to outreach to specific segments of the community if you don't have actual experience with the population the program proposes to serve; of course, if you don't, you want to clarify that. Similarly, when requesting funding for a highly technical project that makes use of new ways to engage clients via the Internet, information about the organization's past experience in web-based communications, as well as the qualifications of specific staff members who would be responsible for the project, would be critical to reinforcing your nonprofit's capacity to undertake the proposed project successfully. If you are proposing a collaborative project, you might give examples of other collaborative projects in which your agency has participated and also the successful outcomes derived from those collaborations.

Testimonials and statistics relating to the work of the nonprofit may be incorporated, although they should be kept at a minimum. The organization background component should be primarily an informative and interesting narrative describing the qualifications of your charity. Understand that the funder would probably prefer a summary of the highlights in the nonprofit's history that relate to the project needing funding. In this instance, don't be afraid to use bullet points to highlight items in what would otherwise become very dense narrative.

Don't eat up valuable proposal space with information on your organization's structure or specific details about board members and staff unless such detail is requested. Supporting documents, such as an organization chart and résumés of key staff, can provide this information and add credibility to your proposal, and they should be provided in the proposal's appendixes (see Step Eleven). However, some funders specify what appendixes they will—and will not accept—so you might have to incorporate this information into the background statement. Should this be the case, keep it brief. Summarize how many staff and board members your organization has and also the number of active volunteers engaged with it.

If your organization is too new to have any accomplishments, try focusing on the qualifications of the staff and board to provide some sense of credibility even as a start-up.

Tips for Writing the Organization Background Component

Start with when and why the charity was created. Its mission statement should be front and center in the first or second paragraph. From there, move away from the philosophy of the organization and begin explaining *what it does.*

This is one of the few sections of a proposal that you can create as a boilerplate and use over and over. You may be required to tweak it here and there to highlight items of special interest to a particular funder. Otherwise, this section is fairly standard for most proposals.

Read the following Sample Organization Background Component. Then, using Worksheet 9.1A, gather the information for this section of your organization's proposal. Worksheet 9.1B offers an example. Next, write your own narrative, using the Sample Organization Background Component as a guide. Finally, review your work using the Organization Background Review Questions. You should be able to answer yes to each question.

Sample Organization Background Component

The Some City Senior Center was established as a 501(c)(3) organization in 1994 by a group of six seniors ages 60 to 82 who wanted to create a place with activities and support services that would cater to the specific needs of seniors. We are the largest senior center in Any County, and serve more than 450 older adults each day as they participate in a variety of programs and services offered at the center. Since our inception, we have proudly served over 5,000 seniors in Any County with a variety of program and services.

The mission of our center is to help seniors improve and maintain a healthy and independent lifestyle and to maximize their quality of life, and our four-pronged purpose is as follows.

1. Promote dignity and self-esteem.

2. Foster independence and self-determination.

3. Facilitate social interaction and involvement in community life.

4. Dispel stereotypes and myths about aging.

Our center serves older adults from Some City, Valley Vista, Grove Beach, and Hill Viejo. The last three cities have the highest concentrations of low-income minority older adults in Any County. Of these three cities, Valley Vista has the largest Latino population. Its population is approximately 70% Latino, and of that Latino population, over 50% are monolingual Spanish speaking.

We operate a nonprofit multipurpose facility governed by an active 16-member volunteer board of directors (including three of the organization's founders), and we offer a wide variety of programs at our center to meet even the most discriminating—and sometimes specific—needs of those we serve. Programs offered include preventive health care and education; nutritious in-center and home-delivered meals; crisis intervention; support groups and case management; legal and insurance counseling; housing assistance; employment training and information; transportation; leisure activities; recreation; volunteerism/placement; and social services and referral information. Our multiuse facility makes us unique from the other senior centers in Any County, and allows us to play an even more vital role in our community.

We recently added a state-of-the-art computer lab where ten separate classes are offered (two each day), Monday through Friday. Older adults who specialize in computer technology volunteer as instructors for these courses. Since adding the computer lab, the Center has trained over 250 seniors in how to use a computer as well as how to access the Internet. And because these classes are fee-for-service, it has finally allowed us to solidify our six months of operating reserves. Our agency has had a clean audit for the last eight years, and our fundraising efforts have grown between 10 and 15% since adding our director of development position five years ago. Additionally, we have successfully secured Community Development Block Grants from two cities as well as county funding for three consecutive years.

Currently, over a dozen organizations regularly use the center after hours and on weekends; among them are Jazzercise, Ballroom Dancing, Senior Net computer classes, Legal Aid Society of Any County, Alcoholics Anonymous meetings, Health Access Latinos, and Families of Any County. This translates into well over 150 community meetings and events, as over 3,000 individuals use the Center every year—this is above and beyond our senior services.

WORKSHEET 9.1A:
Organization Background Exercise™

Worksheet 9.1B contains a sample completed exercise. Please use it as an example as you complete this exercise.

[Organization Name]	Accomplishments	Personnel
Location		
Legal status		
Date of founding		
Mission		
Target population		
Programs		
Partnerships		
How unique		
Special recognition		
Summary of need statement		
Financial		
Board and staff		

WORKSHEET 9.1B:
Organization Background Exercise Example

Some City Senior Center	Accomplishments	Personnel
Location • Some City, YZ (USA) Legal status • 501(c)(3) nonprofit, tax-exempt corporation Date of founding • August 1, 1994 Mission • To help seniors improve and maintain a healthy and independent lifestyle and to maximize their quality of life Target population • All seniors aged 60 and up living in Some City, Valley Vista, Grove Beach, and Hill Viejo Programs • Preventive health care and education • Nutritious in-center and home-delivered meals • Crisis intervention • Support groups and case management • Legal and insurance counseling • Housing assistance • Employment training and information • Transportation • Leisure activities • Recreation • Volunteerism/placement • Social services and referral information	• 450 seniors served annually regardless of their income levels and ability to pay from four cities in Any County • Six months of operating reserves secured • Clean annual audit for the last eight years • 92% satisfaction rating from our membership • Awarded the Some City's Shining Star award for leading nonprofit in 2000 • Strategic plan completed and actively in use (2007–2010) • Government funding secured at both the city and county levels	• Active and engaged 16-member board of directors made up of a diverse group of individuals representing the communities we serve • Full-time development professional • Executive director with a five-year track record of success at the center • Over 100 volunteers who donate well over 300 hours of service each month throughout our agency

WORKSHEET 9.1B: Organization Background Exercise Example (Continued)		
Some City Senior Center	**Accomplishments**	**Personnel**
Partnerships • *With numerous organizations that use our facility* How unique • *The only senior center in Any County with a multiuse facility* • *Fee-for-service computer classes specifically designed for seniors* Special recognition Summary of need statement • *In a survey conducted by the Any County Long-Term Care Multilingual Senior Needs Assessment of 2005, only 3.9 of Spanish-speaking older adults surveyed in our four-city service area reported using senior centers; over 50% of the seniors in our service area live below the federal poverty level and are in need of a variety of services.* Financial • *Clean audit for the last eight years* • *Steady increase in fundraising revenue* • *Six months of operating reserve* Board and staff • *Seasoned executive director* • *Board that is not yet fully reflective of the community it serves, but moving actively in that direction*		

Organization Background Review Questions

1. Does the organization background section give the nonprofit credibility by stating its history, specific qualifications, purpose, programs, target population, total number of people served, and major accomplishments?

2. Does the background suggest sources of community support for the proposed program?

3. Does this section highlight any awards received? This can include winning government funding through a competitive process.

Step 10

Writing the Proposal Summary

YOUR PROPOSAL IS now complete—well, almost! The proposal summary does what its title suggests; it literally summarizes the entire proposal, which is no easy feat. In this step you will learn the basics of constructing a solid and, it is to be hoped, compelling summary. Using a worksheet and following examples, you will also write a summary for your own proposal.

Purpose and Content of the Summary

When you want to know what a novel is all about, what do you do? You flip to the back or inside cover, and you read the two- to three-paragraph book summary, which either motivates you to want to read the book or signals that the book probably holds no interest for you. Well, the same premise holds true for grant proposals. A proposal summary—also referred to as an executive summary—is a sneak peek at what your proposal is all about. That means it needs to be good in order to stimulate the program officer's interest in your project.

All proposals of more than five pages in length should contain a summary, and in most cases funders make a summary a required component of the proposal. The summary is a clear, one- to two-page abstract of the proposal. Positioned at the very beginning, it is typically the section written last to make sure that it incorporates all elements of the completed proposal. A proposal summary should contain the following elements:

- Identification of the applicant (your organization)

- The specific purpose of the grant

- The applicant's qualifications to carry out this purpose (the program)

- The anticipated end result

- The total program or project budget and how much the applicant is requesting from the grantmaker to be used toward that amount

Keeping in mind that on average, summaries are succinct (again, one to two pages maximum), you should include each of these elements in one short paragraph—or less, if possible. It is customary to follow the order just given when writing your summary.

A crisp and well-articulated summary helps the reviewer understand the need for the program and the results expected. It paints a picture of the full proposal and entices the reviewer to read more. A poorly written summary will leave the reviewer asking why the program is important, which will hurt its chances of being funded by that foundation or corporation—in fact, it hurts the proposal's chances of even being read. Always keep in mind that program officers have dozens—and in many cases hundreds—of grant proposals to review during a given funding cycle. Do not give them any reason to set your proposal aside.

Writers employ different approaches to the summary. Some will start with the compelling need the program is addressing, whereas others will start by introducing their organization, its reputation and standing, and its overall qualifications. When in doubt, consider following the same order used in your proposal.

If you find that you struggle with writing the proposal summary, know that you are in good company. Even the most seasoned grantwriters sometimes struggle with this section because it demands brevity. It requires the writer to capture the most essential elements of each component of the proposal, in a condensed style—yet in a way that will capture the reader's attention and distinguish this proposal from the pack.

Tips for Writing the Summary

- Decide what the key points are in each section of the proposal you have been writing throughout this workbook. Include only those key points in the summary.

- Stress the key points that you know are important to the funder. Make sure the summary highlights the potential grantmaker's priorities.

Study the following Sample Summary for the Senior Latino Community Outreach Pilot Project. Then complete Worksheet 10.1A to pull together the material for your summary, using the example in Worksheet 10.1B as a guide. Next, write the summary for your own proposal, consulting the senior center Sample Summary once again. Finally, review your work by asking the Summary Review Questions. You should be able to answer yes to each question.

Sample Summary

The Some City Senior Center was established as a 501(c)(3) organization in 1994 by a group of six seniors ages 60 to 82 who wanted to create a place with activities and support services that would cater to the specific needs of seniors. The Center addresses the health, social, recreational, and logistical needs of the elderly population in four cities. We are the largest senior center in Any County and serve more than 450 older adults each day through a wide variety of programs. Our mission is to help seniors improve and maintain a healthy and independent lifestyle and to maximize their quality of life.

We are conscious of the changing demographics in our center's service area and are committed to growing and adapting our center to meet the emerging needs. The Senior Latino Community Outreach Pilot Project will provide comprehensive access to health and social services to the seniors in the Latino communities served by our center. Program objectives include ensuring that a minimum of 75 Spanish-speaking seniors with Type II diabetes maintain stabilized blood sugar levels for three consecutive months; increasing by 50% the number of monolingual Spanish-speaking seniors who access the services of our center for the first time within the grant period; engaging a minimum of 50 Latino seniors in our new healthy Mexican food cooking class; and increasing our referrals of Latino seniors from the community clinics and partnering nonprofit organizations specifically serving the Latino community by 50% within the grant period. After the pilot phase of the program has been completed, we are committed to phasing in access to our center's other programs.

The Center plays a vital role in the lives of seniors in Some City, Valley Vista, Grove Beach, and Hill Viejo as evidenced by our 92% approval rating from our clients in 2007. These four cities account for 39.8% of Any County's total senior population (which is 15.2% of the county's total population). Our four-city service area has a rapidly growing older adult population, which has nearly doubled since 2000 and is expected to double again over the next two decades. Nearly 50% of our seniors are living below the federal poverty line, and it is estimated that cumulatively, Latino seniors—both bilingual and monolingual—make up an ever-growing segment of total senior population in our service area.

We believe that this project will introduce our center and services to an extremely underserved senior population. As a result, we anticipate a rise in Type II diabetes self-management, fewer seniors who have no medical home, increased diversity among our clients to reflect the changing demographics of the cities we serve, and improved quality of life for those clients.

The total cost of implementation of our Senior Latino Community Outreach Pilot Project is $190,000. Of this amount, $140,000 has already been committed from both county and city governments and other funders. Your investment of $50,000 will complete the funding we need to fully implement this pilot project, and we are excited about the prospect of partnering with you. Thank you for your consideration of our request.

Helpful Hint

Be consistent. Now is not the time to introduce new information. Everything in this section should already be part of your full proposal.

WORSHEET 10.1A:
Summary Questionnaire

Worksheet 10.1B contains sample answers to these questions. Please use it as an example as you complete this questionnaire.

1. What is the identity of your organization, and what is its mission?

2. What is the proposed program or project (title, purpose, target population)?

3. Why is the proposed program or project important?

4. What will be accomplished by this program or project during the time period of the grant?

5. Why should your organization do the program or project (credibility statement)?

6. How much will the program or project cost during the grant time period? How much is being requested from this funder?

WORKSHEET 10.1B:
Summary Questionnaire Example

1. What is the identity of your organization, and what is its mission?

   The Some City Senior Center was established in 1994. We are the largest senior center in Any County. Our center's mission is to help seniors improve and maintain a healthy and independent lifestyle and to maximize their quality of life.

2. What is the proposed program or project (title, purpose, target population)?

   Senior Latino Community Outreach Pilot Project. This project is our first major outreach effort to serve the Latino community of elders—both Spanish and English speaking—with health and social services. We will focus on the seniors living in our service area of Some City, Valley Vista, Grove Beach, and Hill Viejo.

3. Why is the proposed program or project important?

   Because this growing segment of the senior population in Any County is being ignored. In Any County, 37% of Spanish-speaking adults reported income below the federal poverty level. In Valley Vista alone, the population is approximately 70% Latino, and of that Latino group, over 50% are monolingual Spanish speaking.

4. What will be accomplished by this program or project during the time period of the grant?

   The Senior Latino Community Outreach Pilot Project has four goals: (1) increase by 50% the number of monolingual Spanish-speaking seniors who access our services for the first time, (2) engage a minimum of 50 Latino seniors in our new Mexican food healthy cooking classes, (3) increase referrals of Latino seniors to our center from our partnering agencies by 50%, and (4) to graduate a minimum of 75 monolingual Spanish-speaking seniors from our diabetes Type II self-management class, resulting in stabilized blood sugar levels for these individuals for three consecutive months.

5. Why should your organization implement the program or project (credibility statement)?

   We are the largest senior center in Any County, and we have a 92% satisfaction rate from our clients. We have served seniors 60 and up since 1994 and now assist over 450 seniors every single day with their health, social, recreational, and emotional needs so that they can maintain a healthy and independent lifestyle and maximize their quality of life.

6. How much will the program or project cost during the grant time period? How much is being requested from this funder?

   This project has a budget of $190,000, of which all but $50,000 has been secured from government, individual, and foundation sources. The request to this funder is for the remaining $50,000.

Summary Review Questions

1. Does the summary clearly identify the applicant(s)?

2. Does it describe the specific need to be addressed and the specific objectives to be achieved?

3. Does it mention the total program or project cost and the amount of funding requested?

4. Is it brief (no more than one page)?

5. Does it thank the funder for considering the applicant's request for funding?

Moving into the home stretch, you are now ready to put the proposal package together—which just happens to be Step Eleven.

Step 11

Putting the Package Together

IN THIS STEP you will learn the importance of presenting your proposal with a clear but brief cover letter and the attachments that funders may require you to include.

Purpose and Content of the Cover Letter

Your proposal is complete—you did it! Now you need to package it and send it off to the funder. Sounds simple? Well, not so fast. First, you need to craft a brief, yet informative cover letter that will serve as the first piece of information the program officer reads. This letter should accomplish the following:

- Briefly introduce the organization making the request.
- Highlight the support of the board of directors for the project.
- Specifically mention the financial request—how much and for what.

Make it your goal to keep the cover letter to one page and preferably three to four paragraphs maximum. Remember, you have a full and detailed proposal that you want the program officer to read—don't take up her time with an unnecessarily lengthy cover letter. Start the letter by introducing your organization and informing the funder of the amount and purpose of your request. Use the next paragraph to briefly highlight your proposal and any salient points. The closing paragraph should thank the program officer for his consideration of your request and should also clearly indicate whom to contact in your organization with responses. Typically, the person who signs the cover letter—which should be your organization's executive director, board president, or both—is not the contact person who follows up on the request, so make sure to indicate who the contact person is by name and title and to include that person's direct e-mail address and phone extension. Minimize opportunities for confusion, and make it as easy as possible for the foundation representative to reach the right person in your organization.

This final paragraph is also the place to suggest a meeting or invite a site visit between the prospective funder and the applicant to answer questions and provide more information. When the contact person from your organization follows up via e-mail or telephone to confirm receipt of the proposal, that's a great time to again offer the option of a meeting. Use the following Sample Cover Letter as an example.

Sample Cover Letter

Mary Smith, PhD
Program Officer
Community Foundation
4321 Common Lane
Some City, YZ 55555

Dear Dr. Smith:

    The Some City Senior Center is respectfully requesting a grant in the amount of $50,000 for our Senior Latino Community Outreach Pilot Project. As the largest senior center in Any County, serving over 450 seniors every day, we are conscious of the changing demographics in our service area, and are committed to growing and adapting our center to meet emerging needs. The Senior Latino Community Outreach Pilot Project will allow us to pilot a one-year effort to determine if our center can effectively (1) provide comprehensive access to health and social services to seniors in the Latino communities served by our center and (2) raise and fully integrate the cultural competency of the board, staff, and volunteers of the Some City Senior Center.

    Our board of directors is enthusiastic about this program and eager to launch it in an effort to be the most inclusive, responsive, and culturally competent center for seniors in all of our communities that need these services. Should we find at the end of our pilot year that this program is in fact successful, our board is committed to integrating a portion of the project's yearly expenses into our annual operating budget so that the program becomes an integral part of our core services.

    Through this project, the center will serve as the primary referral given by Health Access Latinos, Families of Any County, and three community clinics within a fifteen-mile radius of our center. We will also take referrals of Spanish-speaking seniors from any other community agency in our immediate service area.

    Thank you for your consideration of our request. I will follow up with you in the next week to answer any questions you might have, as well as to learn whether there is a possibility of meeting with you to discuss the merits our proposal. Should you have any questions in the interim, please feel free to contact Connie Jones, our Director of Development, at (555) 555-5555, x555, or cjones@scsc.org.

Sincerely,
Jane Lovely

Purpose and Content of the Appendixes

Appendixes, or attachments, are a necessary and important addition to your grant proposal. They are documents that are not components of the proposal per se yet provide valuable information that the funder will need when considering your request. Most foundation (and government) funders supply a list of their required appendixes, and most corporations do not. When no attachment list is provided, consider including the following documents, unless, of course, the grantmaker specifically says not to:

- Your organization's IRS 501(c)(3) tax-exempt status determination letter or fiscal agent's letter, if there is a sponsor, to establish nonprofit status
- Your organization's most recent audited financial statement
- A list of your organization's board members, their work and school affiliations, and any other applicable information
- Your organization's overall budget for the current fiscal year
- Your organization's latest annual report (if it prepares an annual report)
- A list of all other funders who have received or are receiving proposals for the program, the amounts of these requests, and the current status of each request

In addition to these items, a foundation might request profiles of the key staff members who will be implementing or overseeing the proposed project and a list of current funders. Corporations are typically less likely to want attachments. That said, a copy of your organization's marketing plan and copies of your organization's appearances in the media might be useful to them, as corporations tend to have an interest in receiving public relations exposure for their support. Many foundations—especially those that raise money to fund their grantmaking—increasingly look for information about a nonprofit's marketing and communications capacity, which may influence favorable consideration.

Some funders may also require an attachment section for a letter proposal. Many of the items in the previous list are generally included with these shorter proposals. Letters of intent, however, will most likely require a much reduced appendixes section that includes only the IRS determination letter and possibly a list of members of the board of directors and your organization's budget.

Packaging the Proposal

A simple, clutter-free, and neatly packaged proposal creates the perception of a well-organized, successful organization. Conversely, an envelope full of unorganized pieces of paper does just the opposite. You get only one chance to make a good first impression!

Give your proposal and all appendixes a good "once over" and make sure that

- They are nicely copied on fresh paper.
- The pages are numbered and appropriately identified.
- The proposal is nicely formatted, with no typos (don't rely on spellcheck but run it anyway).
- The name of the foundation, staff person, and address information are correct (and don't hand address the envelope or label).

- The cover letter is printed on your organization's letterhead.

For good measure, and as a way to double-check your work, consider creating a table of contents for your proposal. You might also provide a numbered list of the appendixes, which can then serve as the page separator between your proposal and the attachments section.

Carefully read the funder's guidelines to confirm the number of copies of the proposal that you should send. It is now common for grantmakers to request an original and several copies of a full proposal, so make sure you follow their instructions. If more than one copy of your proposal is requested, clearly mark which proposal is the original. It is also not uncommon for funders to request both a hard copy and an electronic copy via e-mail.

In an effort to cut down on use of paper products in general, proposals (other than letter proposals with only a few appendixes) should be neatly arranged and held together with a large binder clip, rather than a folder. Start with the full proposal, the budget, and then the appendixes *in the order listed in the guidelines.* Leave the cover letter outside the binder clip for your original proposal only. Each copy of your proposal can be fully binder-clipped, with the cover letter copy inside the clip. You can paperclip each section of your proposal if you like (narrative proposal, budget, appendixes), as that might make accessing the proposal overall easier for the funder.

The dress-to-impress strategy does not work when it comes to your proposal. Placing it in a three-ring notebook, having it spiral-bound, or spending unnecessary funds to have it color copied do not add value. Presentation is important, but only from a neatness and orderliness standpoint. Flashy typically backfires—and it ultimately creates more work for the funder, who certainly will not appreciate it.

Use the checklist in Worksheet 11.1 to make sure your proposal is complete and ready to mail.

Reality Check

Broken-record alert. It is essential that you follow the funder's guidelines for packaging your proposal, just as with all other parts of the application process. Nearly all funders—foundations, corporations, and government—will say "no staples." Their staff must take the proposals—dozens or hundreds of them each cycle—apart to make multiple copies for board members to review; staples make their jobs much harder. Use staples and you may immediately disqualify your proposal from consideration—it's that cut and dried. Does the funder ask for twelve-point type, a Times Roman font, and one-inch margins on all sides of the paper? Or maybe the funder wants to receive proposals only on recycled paper, not on your stationery. Whatever the funder has taken the time to specifically outline in its guidelines is exactly what you should give the funder. Do not provide any reason for your proposal to be disqualified.

WORSHEET 11.1:
Final Proposal Checklist

Place a checkmark next to each step after it is completed.

_____ Determine which program or project ideas have the best chance of being funded.

_____ Form a planning team that includes clients affected by the program or project, community leaders, key staff and volunteers, and other organizations with similar or complementary projects.

_____ Design a program or project plan.

_____ Conduct thorough research to determine funding sources most likely to be interested in the program or project. Note funder deadlines.

_____ Visit the website of each prospective funder to review its grant guidelines, annual report, grantee list, and so forth. If a funder has no website, e-mail or call to request information helpful in preparing the proposal (annual report, grant guidelines, and so on).

_____ Read all other grantmaker materials (Form 990, media coverage, and so on) to ensure that the proposal falls within the funder's interest areas as demonstrated by previous grants made.

_____ Prepare the proposal core components by stating the need or problem to be addressed, the objectives and the methods for meeting the need, the ways the project will be evaluated and funded in the future, and the budget.

_____ Determine the features of the program or project that may set it apart from other projects and will appeal to the funder.

_____ Make sure those features are highlighted for the grantmaker.

_____ Prepare the final proposal components: the introduction, summary, and cover letter.

_____ Ensure the proposal is clear and well written by having at least one person review it and provide feedback.

_____ Include the appendixes requested by the funder.

_____ Review grant guidelines and confirm the number of proposal copies to be submitted and any specific formatting requests, in order to meet the requirements.

_____ Give copies of the proposal to members of the planning team and other individuals or groups who should be aware of the program or project.

_____ E-mail or call the funder within two weeks after mailing the proposal.

Sending the Proposal

Congratulations! You have "twelve stepped" your way to a solidly developed grant proposal based on the keys to success discussed in this workbook's Introduction. For a proposal to be successful it must reflect the work of a fully developed and articulated program plan—which is 80 percent of the up-front work and is sometimes easily overlooked. Only then is the proposal written (the other 20 percent), clearly and concisely, for a targeted funder who has been thoroughly researched and vetted and with whom a relationship has been established.

Please pay particular attention to the Special Resource Section at the end of this workbook, where you can find out more about how to research funders and learn about their preferences and values. When your organization's proposal has been packaged and mailed out to prospective funders, go through Step Twelve (the next step in this workbook) to review some suggested strategies for maintaining contact with those funders and moving your proposal through their grantmaking process.

Sustaining Relationships with Funders

YOUR ORGANIZATION CREATED a great program plan that addresses a truly compelling need. Then, following the *Winning Grants Step by Step* twelve-step model, you wrote a stellar grant proposal, and you followed the funder's guidelines when preparing and mailing your full proposal package. Mission accomplished? Well, not quite yet.

Following Up on Your Organization's Proposal

Many funders will say in their grant guidelines that they require a certain number of weeks or months to review all applications, and they will request that organizations not call during that period. In addition, more funders are incorporating site visits into their grantmaking processes, and they want to save all discussion and questions for that time. However, if not specifically mentioned otherwise in their guidelines, it is a good idea to make a follow-up call after a couple of weeks to confirm receipt of your proposal and find out what the next steps are in the process.

Managing a Site Visit

A *site visit* is exactly what its name implies: the funder comes to your organization's *site* (or the site of the proposed program) to *visit* with leaders, staff, board members, and those the organization serves. Not every organization requesting funding gets a site visit, because it is a part of the vetting process for proposals that are in the advanced stage of consideration. You should also understand that a site visit is by no means an assurance of funding for your program. What it does mean is that there is enough of a match between the grantmaker, the organization, and the proposed program that the funder believes it warrants further investigation.

When a site visit is requested, the key staff assigned to the program are essential to the process because they (ideally) were the people who created the program plan, and they are the ones (again, ideally) who will be responsible for the hands-on implementation of the project. They should be present during the visit, as should the executive director and the person who can answer financial or budgetary questions. If the program targets a specific group of people, representation in the form of one or more individuals from the population to be served or engaged is always welcome, as they can provide the most useful testimony for your project, its significance, and its power for change.

If your nonprofit has been selected for a site visit, use the following to-do list to prepare:

- Confirm the participation of all key persons involved with the program.

- Send the full proposal to everyone participating, and request that they (re)familiarize themselves with it.

- If the funder has provided questions in advance of the site visit, share those as well.

- Meet with everyone in advance of the actual site visit to ensure that everyone is on the same page in terms of knowledge about the program and its goals, objectives, and methods and that everyone understands who will be answering which questions and moderating the visit.

- Make sure beverages are available for the visit, but keep it basic: no need for catering or any other "special event" details.

If the grantmaker has requested a tour of some sort, decide what the important elements are for the funder's representatives to see and plan the tour in advance—again informing everyone who will be a part of it what is happening and when. Make sure everything is in order and try to schedule the tour for a time when they can see the programs in action; check with staff to make sure it won't be disruptive to have visitors or violate clients' confidentiality or privacy in any way.

Keeping the Funder Informed

Remember when you prepared your program budget and you mentioned all the other sources you were approaching as well? Keeping prospective funders up to date on which of these other grantmakers has awarded a grant to your program or has declined your request at this time is always recommended. As new grant requests are submitted, you again want to notify all foundations that are currently considering your program that you are approaching additional funders. Refer back to each individual funder's guidelines to be sure you are honoring any requests that that funder has made regarding being open to phone calls and e-mail communication during the review process.

Responding to the Funder's Decision

It is inevitable: funding decisions will be made. When they are, you and your organization's staff will either be jumping for joy or holding your heads in your hands. Believe it or not, you need to move forward with your relationship-building regardless of which way the decision falls.

When the Proposal Is Funded

There is nothing like getting that call, letter, or e-mail informing you that your organization's proposal has been funded. It is the best, regardless of the size of the grant. So after the *yippee*s are shouted, you need to get back to business—remember, you are building a relationship. A telephone call to your program officer is certainly in order as soon as you receive word that your request is being approved. As busy as program officers are, they all want to hear about how the programs—and organizations—they've funded are progressing. In most foundations the process of the grantmaking system requires program officers to advocate for the programs they are recommending for funding. Your program officer has gone to bat on your behalf to get you those funds, so consider her a partner and keep her apprised on a quarterly basis with a brief note, an e-mail, a call, a personalized newsletter, or whatever form of communication you think is most effective and appropriate.

I like when grantees take the initiative to schedule a site visit for me at least once a year. This allows me to be in touch, without feeling overbearing or intrusive, and to feel like I am doing a better job of monitoring my docket. Also, I really appreciate it when a grantee calls me to get input on an organizational issue they may be facing during the course of their project. It helps me to stay connected with the organization, and to understand how the project is proceeding. Then when I get the regular written evaluations of the grants, I am seldom surprised by anything in it. I have always thought that if a funded project didn't change during the life of the grant from what was anticipated during the application stage, then something was seriously awry in either the implementation of the project, or the reporting on it.

—GWEN I. WALDEN

Principal, Walden Philanthropy Advisors

Former Director, Center for Healthy Communities

The California Endowment

Following your telephone call to the program officer—and within three to five days of notification—you need to send a formal letter of thanks to the funder that is signed by the executive director or the board chair, or both.

In general, funders expect some sort of public recognition of their grants. Standard forms of recognition include a feature in the grantee's newsletter and inclusion on a donor list on the recipient's website or in the annual report. Consider the level of recognition in proportion to the amount of funds received; that should guide you toward choosing the appropriate recognition level. A large grant may warrant special recognition at your organization's annual event, if there is one, a ceremony of some sort, or a media announcement. Ultimately, if anything beyond a newsletter mention and inclusion in your donor list is being considered, it should be discussed with the funder in advance of making any decisions. You do not want your organization to engage in "surprise" or unwanted donor recognition.

If the funding institution (or the grant) is to remain anonymous, the funder will clearly stipulate that fact in its grant award letter to you. Of course in such situations the funder's name should not be mentioned anywhere publicly, and care should be taken in all internal records to mark the grant-maker as anonymous.

When a grant is awarded, the nonprofit will

- Receive initial notification of the award, usually informally through a phone call or e-mail.

- Receive official confirmation in the form of a *grant agreement* letter.

- Have your organization's executive director and other appropriate staff (such as the person responsible for program implementation and the person responsible for organization finances) review this document to ensure that the nonprofit will be able to comply with all of its stipulations, as it is a legally binding agreement.

- Return the letter—signed by the executive director—within three to five days of receipt.

- Provide quarterly, semiyearly, or yearly progress reports. Each funder has different requirements, but these will be spelled out clearly in the grant agreement letter. Timely reports are especially critical if the non-profit hopes to be eligible to reapply to this funder for further support.

Notify the funder of all major changes or issues you have identified in your program as soon as possible. Staffing changes, a particular method that is not working, and participant recruitment that is well below what was originally targeted—these are all examples of situations about which your funding partner should be informed.

When the Proposal Is Not Funded

Your mail comes and there it is: an envelope from the funder. Upon reading it you find that your proposal was not approved. There will be dozens—and in some cases hundreds—of other organizations just like yours that receive the same declination letter. So what happened? Why was your organization's program not selected? On average, a typical foundation can make grants in response to approximately 8 to 10 percent of the total requests it receives in every funding cycle. Sometimes the approval rate is even significantly lower than that, especially for the largest foundations in the United States.

Your organization's declination letter will likely be very general and provide you with only vague reasons for the denial. So you might want to follow up with your program officer via e-mail to see if you can get more detail as to why your organization's proposal was not funded. Consider asking the following three questions in your e-mail:

- Were there any parts of the funder's guidelines that you missed? (You want to find out up front if your proposal was disqualified for any reason.)

- Was additional information or further clarity needed in your program plan or grant proposal to make it more competitive?

- Is it recommended that you resubmit this proposal for consideration at another time? If so, when?

You also want to thank the funder for considering your request and for taking the time to respond to your e-mail. Let politeness be the rule, and remember that there is always the next cycle.

The reality is this: there are many stellar programs that do not get funded. There are compelling grant proposals that do not get funded. The demand for foundation and corporate (and government) grants is simply too high—and competition for these dollars grows more stiff each and every year.

So how can you make your organization, program, and proposal stand out? Be organized, truthful, respectful, consistent, and persistent in your grantseeking endeavors. It is vital that you keep in mind that a denial from a funder does not mean that your program lacks merit, nor does it mean that your program will never get funded.

There are more reasons than pages in this workbook that might explain why the funder has denied your proposal; just continue building your relationships. Consider keeping all the funders you've identified as a match for your programs—even if they have denied your request for funding—on your mailing list; also invite them to your events, and continue to share

---

Reality Check

Be persistent. One human service organization in Northern California was turned down by a certain local foundation well over a half dozen times but continued to cultivate a relationship with the program officer over a five-year period. When the foundation launched an initiative that happened to be closely aligned with the nonprofit's mission and purpose, the program officer actually initiated contact with the nonprofit, because they now had a relationship. And you know what happened next. The nonprofit submitted a proposal and was funded—and has a relationship with that funder to this day.

---

organization successes with them via periodic updates through e-mails and other communications.

The takeaways from *Winning Grants Step by Step, Third Edition,* are twofold. First, we wanted to provide you with the time-tested, nuts and bolts of proposal development and a framework for how they should come together. Much of the material in the second edition also remains relevant now—it works. Second, we wanted to provide some additional context for the grantseeking process itself. As we have mentioned in several places in this workbook, a well-written, well-organized grant proposal is a critical component of the funding equation, but there is more you need to do to ultimately "win" that grant. We wanted to provide you with the knowledge that grantseeking is a process that in many cases spans months—and in some cases years—of cultivation and relationship building.

In other words: grantseeking is a marathon—not a sprint.

Special Resource Section

Resource A

Types of Foundations

STEP TWO took you through the logic and strategy of developing relationships with funders. This resource provides you with a brief "101" on the various types of foundations:

Community foundation. A community foundation is a tax-exempt, nonprofit, autonomous, publicly supported, nonsectarian philanthropic institution with a long-term goal of building permanent, named component funds, established by many separate donors, for the broad-based charitable benefit of the residents of a defined geographic area, typically no larger than a state.

Corporate foundation. Also referred to as a *company-sponsored foundation,* a corporate foundation is established by a corporation but tends to operate separately from the company and to have its own dedicated staff. In most cases it is a separate legal entity that maintains close ties to the parent company, and the members of the foundation and company boards can overlap. These foundations tend to give to a broad spectrum of organizations; however, some establish giving policies that reflect the parent company's interest. Often, corporate foundations provide grant support in the areas where their corporation has a base of operation.

Donor-advised fund. A donor-advised fund (DAF) "is a charitable giving vehicle set up under the tax umbrella of a public charity, which acts as sponsor to many funds. A donor-advised fund offers the opportunity to create an easy-to-establish, low cost, flexible vehicle for charitable giving as an alternative to direct giving or creating a private foundation. Donors enjoy administrative convenience, cost savings and tax advantages by conducting their grantmaking through a donor-advised fund." Once the primary domain of community foundations, DAFs are now being offered at major financial institutions such as Fidelity Investments, which has the largest DAF program in the country. DAFs are now the fastest growing charitable vehicle, with over 100,000 DAFs holding over $17.5 billion in assets.[1] Unfortunately for grantseekers, nonprofits typically cannot apply for these funds, as the grants are recommended by the advisers to the funds.

Family foundation. "The term 'family foundation' does not have any legal meaning, but the Council on Foundations defines a family foundation as one in which the donor or the donor's relatives play a significant role in governing and/or managing the foundation."[2]

Operating foundation. An operating foundation is a private foundation that uses its resources to conduct research or provide a direct service. It is not uncommon for this type of foundation to engage in fundraising as a means of generating the revenue it needs to make grants.

Private foundation. Also referred to as an *independent foundation,* a private foundation is a nongovernmental, noncorporate, nonprofit organization with an endowment and a program managed by its own trustees or directors. The endowment has usually been donated by a single source, such as an individual, family, or corporation, and this donor also defines the mission and the program of the foundation.

Public foundation. Also referred to as a grantmaking public charity. These are foundations that raise money from the public—individuals, corporations, and other foundations—to provide grants. The IRS does not consider these as private foundations since their base of support is typically broad. Community foundations are recognized as public foundations, as are women's funds (www.wfnet.org) and some health care conversion funds.

Notes

1. Definition from Wikipedia, http://en.wikipedia.org/wiki/Donor_advised _funds.

2. Definition from the Foundation Center, http://foundationcenter.org/ getstarted/topical/family.html.

Resource B

How to Research Funders

THE VAST MAJORITY of prospect research for funding institutions that best match your organization's programs can be done in the comfort of your own office by using the Internet.

The Foundation Center (http://foundationcenter.org) will probably be the very first stop on your prospect research journey, as it remains one of the primary sources of information on the field of philanthropy.[1] The center's online description of its role in philanthropy is as follows:

> *Established in 1956, and today supported by more than 600 foundations, the Foundation Center is the nation's leading authority on philanthropy, connecting nonprofits and the grantmakers supporting them to tools they can use and information they can trust. The Center maintains the most comprehensive database on U.S. grantmakers and their grants—a robust, accessible knowledge bank for the sector. It also operates research, education, and training programs designed to advance philanthropy at every level. The Center's Web site receives more than 47,000 visits each day, and thousands of people gain access to free resources in its five regional library/learning centers and its national network of more than 340 Cooperating Collections.*

You can access some basic information from the Foundation Center's website for free, including each private foundation's IRS Form 990-PF. (This form, which assesses compliance with the Internal Revenue Code, lists the organization's assets, receipts, expenditures, and compensation of directors and officers, and it lists grants awarded during the previous year.)

That said, you should be aware that this information (from the Foundation Finder section of the site) is very preliminary, consisting of contact information, type of foundation, IRS exemption status, financial data, and employer identification number (EIN).

The detailed data—the data that will tell you about a foundation's funding priorities, past grants it has made with more information available than in the Form 990-PF listing, annual report information, and the rest—is available for a fee through a Foundation Center resource, the Foundation Directory Online (http://fconline.fdncenter.org). According to the website of the Foundation Directory Online, it offers "the most comprehensive, in-depth information available on U.S. grantmakers and their grants, drawn from reliable sources, including IRS 990s, grantmaker websites and annual reports, plus data provided directly by grantmakers—ensuring the most accurate, timely information possible."

The Foundation Directory Online has the potential to cut down on the amount of time you need to dedicate to the compilation of information. Instructions are provided, and the website walks you through its use.

FC Search is another research option provided by the Foundation Center. It is the database on a CD-ROM, a portable research tool that provides access to over ninety-one thousand foundations, corporate donors, and public charities.

Two other websites worthy of mention are BIG Online (www.bigonline.com) and Foundation Search America (www.foundationsearch.com). Both are popular resources made available to nonprofits for a fee. These for-profit web-based resources provide online and telephone assistance for navigating the various tools available on the website, online classes to learn more about the various features of the database and website, access to grantmaker 990's, and a database of relevant articles. These websites also offer the ability to conduct in-depth analysis of prospective foundations.

If it happens that you do not have Internet access, locate your closest Cooperating Collection. Cooperating Collections are free funding information centers in libraries, community foundations, and other nonprofit resource centers that provide a core collection of Foundation Center publications and a variety of supplementary materials and services in areas useful to grantseekers.

If you both lack Internet access and are not close to a Cooperating Collection, then check out your local library. At minimum, libraries will have the printed Foundation Center directories for you to use.

Regardless of the road you travel with your prospect research, it should lead to this:

- The identification of prospect foundations and corporations—those whose interests most closely match what you are seeking to fund.

- A comprehensive understanding of the specific interests of each prospect so that you can target each proposal accordingly.

- The identification of any connections between your organization and one or more prospect foundations or corporations; the connection might be through someone who is on your organization's board of directors or staff or who is a volunteer or donor.

Here are some steps to online funder research:

1. Identify the search criteria you want to use in advance of starting your research. These can include key words, subject matter, geographic area, target audience, gender, race and ethnicity, and any other criteria that fit your interests. Doing this in advance will help you in refining and targeting your research.

2. Using the subject index of each directory, look up your predetermined subject areas and type of support indexes (new program, capital, general operating, and so on). Those foundations and corporations that fund within the type of support you are seeking and that also express an interest in one or more of your subject areas are likely your strongest prospects. Keep an eye out for funders located in your geographic area, as they are the ones most likely to give close consideration to your proposal.

3. Study the information on each prospect you have identified to learn all you can about it, as this will allow you to further determine whether there is truly a match.

4. Once you have identified those funding sources that best match your program's funding needs, visit their websites and get to know them even more. Review their annual reports, success stories of previous grants made, staff biographies, and everything else they are sharing with the public. Visiting each prospect funder's website to check guidelines is also a critical step because guidelines do change over time—and sometimes the changes are significant—but the changes may not have made their way yet into the online directory.

5. With all the information obtained from your prospects' websites, you can get a much clearer sense of how to target your proposals to "speak" to each funder in a language to which its program officer will likely relate. You will also have a grasp on how much you can reasonably request from each funder.

6. Create a prospect grid that lists every prospect identified; the program of your organization that most closely aligns with each prospect's funding interests as outlined in its grant guidelines; your proposed request amount; deadline dates; and all other pertinent information. Pass this prospect list around to your board and staff to determine

whether anyone has a personal contact on the board or staff of any of these prospect funders.

Here are a few additional, and more creative, ways to identify funder prospects:

1. Visit the websites of nonprofit organizations that are similar to your organization in their mission, geographic area, or target audience and take a look at their donor pages. Once you get the names of the foundations that have supported them, use an Internet search engine to find out more about these funders.

2. Survey your surroundings. Are there any corporate headquarters close by? Or maybe franchise outlets of popular chains (of restaurants, retail stores, conveniences stores, and the like)? Contact their corporate headquarters, and find out about their corporate contribution programs—for both funding grants and in-kind support.

3. Look on the donor walls of your local hospitals, universities, and museums. Make note of the foundations and corporations that support these institutions, and then look them up online to find out more. Who knows? You just might find a match, especially if your organization is of the same type.

4. Go to the Forum of Regional Associations of Grantmakers (www .givingforum.org) to locate your local regional association of grantmakers, and then visit that local association's website to see what resources and leads it might provide.

5. See if you can set up a meeting with the donor relations staff person at your community foundation. Your goal is to find out more about the donor-advised funds it has and to see if you can identify potential matches for your program, areas where your organization's interests match a donor adviser's interests.

Note

1. *Philanthropy:* (1) Voluntary action for the public good. (2) Love of humankind, usually expressed by an effort to enhance the well-being of humanity through personal acts of practical kindness or by financial support of a cause or causes. (3) Any effort to relieve human misery or suffering, improve the quality of life, encourage aid or assistance, or foster preservation of values through gifts, service, or other voluntary activity.

Resource C

Sample Logic Model

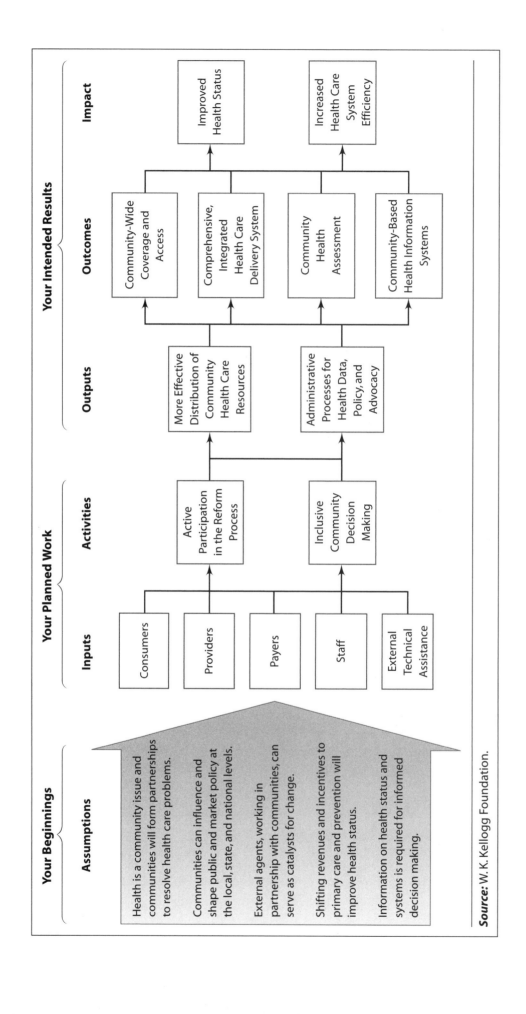

Source: W. K. Kellogg Foundation.

Making the Call

by Sarah S. Brophy

A CRITICAL PIECE of proposal writing isn't writing at all, it's talking. If you haven't called to speak to a foundation officer or program director before preparing a proposal, you risk wasting your time writing it and someone's time reading it.

Most of our initial donor information comes from print and electronic publications that could be out of date, or worse, gathered without the donor's input. It could be grievously wrong, or just slightly. You could be applying for the right program with the wrong audience, or the right project and the wrong amount of money. A discussion with their staff will help you craft a more responsive and complete proposal, and improve your chance of success. This call is not for reconnaissance; that's done during preliminary research. Collect all the information you can; then call the foundation only if you see no reason not to apply, or if you have a question about a specific requirement that you cannot answer through your own research.

Before picking up the phone, practice your elevator-ride speech. This survivor of the early days of venture capital is your thirty-second sales pitch. Develop and practice it before making the call—write it out in case your courage fails you or your mind goes blank.

Tell whomever answers: "I'm Sarah Brophy from the Carlisle Historical Society. I've read your guidelines and Form 990, and visited your website. I believe our project matches your interests, but I would like to be sure before I submit a proposal. May I speak with a program officer about the appropriateness of the project and its components?"

Reprinted from S. S. Brophy, "Making the Call," *Grants & Foundations Review* (CharityChannel e-newsletter), Apr. 2, 2002 (http://two.charitychannel.com/publish/templates/?a=365&z=0).

Then they know you have done your homework and will let you past the front line. When you reach the officer explain: "I'm Sarah Brophy from the Carlisle Historical Society. We are considering applying to Tacoma Foundation for support of a community restoration project for our historic graveyard. We work with professional stone conservators to train high school students, adult volunteers and the Town's department of public works in identification, assessment and care of these 18th century burial markers. Seventy-five percent of the stones have suffered from weather and vandalism and lie broken or buried in the graveyard. Our five month training and conservation project will record and restore 81 stones, provide volunteers and town staff with training for ongoing maintenance, cultivate adult supporters of historic preservation, and encourage students to value and protect this site."

If you are pretty sure how much you will ask for, say "The project costs $xxxxx and we would like to ask the Tacoma Foundation to consider $xxxxx in support of this project." If you are not quite sure the project is appropriate, say "Do you have time to speak with me about the appropriateness of this project?"

You will have answered the who, what, when, where, how and why. Now it's their turn to ask specific questions and then recommend whether or not you should apply, and how to apply. (Of course this means you have to understand the project entirely before making the call, and have a backup project if you miss the mark.) Be ready to answer questions like:

- Which of your personnel would be involved?

- How much it will cost?

- What are the goals and the outcomes?

- Can you replicate it?

- Would it be better done with a partner?

- Has anyone else done this? (Why or why not).

- Why are you the best to do this?

- If it involves construction, know all the permits needed, start and end dates, estimated amounts, any contingency fund, and will you have to borrow?

- Whom else are you asking to fund this?

It's okay to ask how competitive the project might be. They'll explain that every pool is different, but that generally this type of project scores well (or does not). They have no time to waste reading ill-fitting proposals so they will give you a fair answer. If the answer is "You are certainly welcome to apply, but . . ." don't. If they encourage you to apply, do confirm the dates and the contact name.

Foundation officers and government program directors are in the business of finding good ways to share their wealth. They want the best matches possible. Your intelligent, efficient presentation is an excellent introduction for your organization. Even if this project doesn't work out, your professionalism will be appreciated and will help you next time you call.

Remember to thank them for their time. They work hard too, you know.

Resource E

Bibliography

Brophy, S. "Making the Call." *Grants & Foundations Review* (CharityChannel e-newsletter). [http://two.charitychannel.com/publish/templates/?a=365&z=0], Apr. 2, 2002.

Browning, B. *Grant Writing for Dummies.* (2nd ed.) Hoboken, N.J.: Wiley, 2005.

Capek, M., and Mead, M. *Effective Philanthropy.* Cambridge, Mass.: MIT Press, 2006.

Council on Foundations. Website. [http://www.cof.org], 2008.

Dorothy A. Johnson Center for Philanthropy & Nonprofit Leadership. *Nonprofit Good Practice Guide.* [http://www.npgoodpractice.org], 2008.

Foundation Center. *What Is a Foundation.* New York: Foundation Center, 2008.

Kiritz, N. *Program Planning and Proposal Writing.* Los Angeles: Grantsmanship Center, 1980.

Quick, J. A., and New, C. C. *Grant Seeker's Budget Toolkit.* Hoboken, N.J.: Wiley, 2001.

Robinson, A. *Grassroots Grants: An Activist's Guide to Grantseeking.* (2nd ed.) Hoboken, N.J.: Wiley, 2004.

Wason, S. D. *Webster's New World Grant Writing Handbook.* Hoboken, N.J.: Wiley, 2004.

W. K. Kellogg Foundation. *Evaluation Handbook.* [http://www.wkkf.org/DesktopModules], 1998.

W. K. Kellogg Foundation. *Logic Model Development Guide.* [http://www.wkkf.org/DesktopModules], 2004.

Resource F

Helpful Websites for Grantseekers

Alliance for Nonprofit Management: www.allianceonline.org

A professional association of individuals and organizations devoted to improving the management and governance capacity of nonprofits to assist them in fulfilling their mission.

American Association of Grant Professionals: http://go-aagp.org

A nonprofit membership association that builds and supports an international community of grant professionals committed to serving the greater public good by practicing the highest ethical and professional standards.

Association of Fundraising Professionals: www.afpnet.org

An association working to advance philanthropy through advocacy, research, education, and certification programs.

Big Online: www.bigdatabase.com

A comprehensive source of fundraising information, opportunities, and resources for charities and nonprofits.

Board Match Plus: www.boardmatchplus.org

A resource offering an online matching process to organizations seeking board members and to individuals seeking board positions.

BoardSource: www.boardsource.org

A resource for building effective nonprofit boards.

CharityChannel.com: www.CharityChannel.com

A subscription resource that connects you to your nonprofit colleagues across town, across the country, and around the world.

Chronicle of Philanthropy: **www.philanthropy.com**

A newspaper to the nonprofit world.

CompassPoint: www.compasspoint.org

A nonprofit consulting and training organization that provides nonprofits with concepts and management tools to facilitate excellence in community services.

Council on Foundations: www.cof.org

An organization that addresses important issues and challenges facing foundation and corporate funders.

European Foundation Centre: www.efc.be

An international, not-for-profit association promoting and supporting the work of active European foundations.

Forum of Regional Associations of Grantmakers: www.givingforum.org

A national philanthropic leader and a network of thirty-two regional associations of grantmakers.

Foundation Center: www.foundationcenter.org

The Center maintains a comprehensive database on U.S. grantmakers and their grants.

Foundation Search America: www.foundationsearch.com

An online resource including more than 120,000 foundations and tools to locate grants by type, value, year, etc.

Funders Online: www.fundersonline.org

A source of information on foundations and corporate funders active in Europe; also provides links to Europe's online philanthropic community.

Fundsnet Services Online: www.fundsnetservices.com

A source of information on grants, fundraising, and philanthropy resources.

The Grantsmanship Center: www.tgci.com

A training and resource center that provides links to U.S. and international funding sources.

GuideStar: www.guidestar.org

A resource that offers a searchable database of over 1.7 million U.S. nonprofit organizations, including foundations.

Idealist: www.idealist.org

A project of Action Without Borders, active in 153 countries, providing an extensive offering of services related to all aspects of nonprofit development, organization, and management.

National Center for Charitable Statistics: http://nccs.urban.org

The national clearinghouse for data on the nonprofit sector in the United States.

National Endowment for the Arts: www.arts.endow.gov

A website that serves as a comprehensive resource for funding the arts, with links and foundation information.

The Nonprofit Good Practice Guide: www.npgoodpractice.org

A resource that provides easily accessible and continuously updated information on virtually all aspects of managing a nonprofit organization.

***The NonProfit Times:* www.nptimes.com**

A business publication for nonprofit management.

Philanthropy News Network: www.pnnonline.org

A website with information for the nonprofit sector.

***Town & Country* magazine: www.townandcountrymag.com**

A "lifestyles of the rich and famous" publication that dedicates its December issue every year to philanthropy.

The Urban Institute: www.urban.org

A nonprofit public policy research organization in Washington, D.C., useful for statistical data.

USA.gov for Nonprofits: http://www.usa.gov/Business/Nonprofit.shtml

A government website that provides links to federal government information and services for nonprofits, including grant information.

Women's Funding Network: www.wfnet.org

An international organization with over 100 member funds that are committed to improving the status of women and girls.

Government Grant Opportunities

Catalog of Federal Domestic Assistance: http://12.46.245.173/cfda/cfda.html

A database that lists all federal programs available to state and local governments (including the District of Columbia); federally recognized Indian tribal governments; territories (and possessions) of the United States; domestic public, quasi-public, and private for-profit and nonprofit organizations and institutions; specialized groups; and individuals.

Grants.gov: www.grants.gov

A source, managed by the U.S. Department of Health and Human Services, for finding and applying for various federal government grants.

U.S. Department of Education (ED): www.ed.gov/fund/landing.jhtml

A website that offers information on ED grants and contracts.

U.S. Department of Housing and Urban Development (HUD): www.hud.gov/grants/index.cfm

A website that offers information on HUD awards and grants to organizations and groups for a variety of purposes.

Index

How to Use the CD-ROM

System Requirements

PC with Microsoft Windows 98SE or later

Mac with Apple OS version 10.1 or later

Using the CD With Windows

To view the items located on the CD, follow these steps:

1. Insert the CD into your computer's CD-ROM drive.

2. A window appears with the following options:

   Contents: Allows you to view the files included on the CD.

   Software: Allows you to install useful software from the CD.

   Links: Displays a hyperlinked page of websites.

   Author: Displays a page with information about the author(s).

   Contact Us: Displays a page with information on contacting the publisher or author.

   Help: Displays a page with information on using the CD.

   Exit: Closes the interface window.

If you do not have autorun enabled, or if the autorun window does not appear, follow these steps to access the CD:

1. Click Start → Run.

2. In the dialog box that appears, type d:\start.exe, where d is the letter of your CD-ROM drive. This brings up the autorun window described in the preceding set of steps.

3. Choose the desired option from the menu. (See Step 2 in the preceding list for a description of these options.)

In Case of Trouble

If you experience difficulty using the CD, please follow these steps:

1. Make sure your hardware and systems configurations conform to the systems requirements noted under "System Requirements" above.

2. Review the installation procedure for your type of hardware and operating system. It is possible to reinstall the software if necessary.

To speak with someone in Product Technical Support, call 800-762-2974 or 317-572-3994 Monday through Friday from 8:30 a.m. to 5:00 p.m. EST. You can also contact Product Technical Support and get support information through our website at www.wiley.com/techsupport.

Before calling or writing, please have the following information available:

- Type of computer and operating system.

- Any error messages displayed.

- Complete description of the problem.

It is best if you are sitting at your computer when making the call.

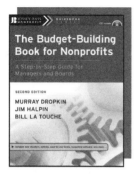

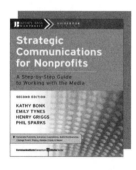

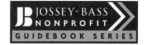